D1624403

Currency Swaps

CURRENCY SWAPS

Brian Coyle

Glenlake Publishing Company, Ltd
Chicago • London • New Delhi

AMACOM
American Management Association

New York • Atlanta • Boston • Chicago • Kansas City • San Francisco • Washington, D.C.
Brussels • Mexico City • Tokyo • Toronto

This book is available at a special
discount when ordered in bulk quantities.
For information contact Special Sales Department,
AMACOM, an imprint of AMA Publications, a division of
American Management Association,
1601 Broadway, New York, NY 10019

ISBN: 0-8144-0615-7

Printing number

10 9 8 7 6 5 4 3 2 1

Contents

Introduction

Swaps originated in the 1970s and have become an important financial instrument for debt management and interest rate risk management. The swaps market was developed by, and is still dominated by, the major commercial and investment banks which actively market their products and services to corporate, institutional and government clients.

A swap is a contract between two counterparties who agree to exchange a stream of payments over an agreed period of several years.

Types of Swap

There are several types of swap

- equity swaps (or equity-linked swaps)
- commodity swaps
- credit swaps.

In an equity swap, the two counterparties exchange a stream of payments based on the performance of an underlying quantity of equity shares or an equity share index.

A commodity swap is an agreement in which the counterparties exchange cash flows based on the price of a commodity, such as jet fuel oil, other grades of fuel oil, and natural gas. One counterparty pays a fixed price on an underlying quantity of the commodity and the other pays a floating price, usually based on the commodity's average price over a period.

Credit swaps are of two main types

- currency swaps
- interest rate swaps.

A credit swap involves an exchange of interest payments based on an amount of principal, and in the case of currency swaps, there is usually also an exchange of principal amounts. A distinction is also made, for credit swaps, between

- liability swaps, and
- asset swaps.

A liability swap involves the exchange of payments on one debt (liability) for payments on another. It enables a borrower to modify his liabilities, for example to exchange a fixed-rate liability for a floating-rate liability or the liability on a debt in one currency for a liability in another currency. Liability swaps therefore are an instrument for debt/liability management.

An asset swap is used to exchange a stream of income from one investment (asset) for income from an alternative source. The structure of a liability swap and an asset swap are the same. The terms are used to distinguish the *purpose* of the swap.

Liability swaps are more common than asset swaps, and the term 'liability swap' is rarely applied to a currency swap. A currency swap is presumed to be a liability swap unless it is called an asset swap.

Credit swaps therefore can be grouped into four main categories.

Types of Credit Swap

Interest rate liability swaps	**Interest rate asset swaps**
Currency (liability) swaps	**Currency asset swaps**

This book deals with currency asset and liability swaps.

Features of Currency Swaps

A currency swap is the exchange of obligations to pay interest and repay principal in one currency in exchange for receiving interest and principal in a second currency.

The Swap Mechanism

A currency swap is a legal agreement consisting of at least two of the following elements

- an arrangement to buy or sell a given quantity of one currency in exchange for another, at an agreed rate on a stipulated date (the near-value date), usually at the spot exchange rate (less typically at a forward or other stipulated rate)
- a simultaneous arrangement to re-exchange the same quantity of currency, usually at exactly the same exchange rate, at a stipulated date in the medium- to long-term (the far-value date that is at the swap's maturity)
- a settlement for interest costs between the two parties for the duration of the swap, payable either at regular intervals (or six monthly or annually) or in a single settlement at maturity.

The settlements for interest costs can involve either a two-way exchange of interest payments in each currency, or a single settlement of the difference between the two amounts in one of the currencies to the swap. For example, if Alpha and Beta swap liabilities in dollars and sterling, the exchange of interest payments might involve the regular payments of interest in sterling by Alpha to Beta in exchange for interest in dollars from Beta to Alpha. Less commonly used is an arrangement whereby on each interest exchange date either Alpha or Beta makes a single payment in dollars or sterling to the other, as a settlement for the difference in interest rates.

The purpose of these interest payments is to ensure that the finance costs of each party are covered.

These three elements in a swap are illustrated on page 8. The currencies shown in the illustration are dollars and sterling.

Currency swaps need not involve an exchange of principal at the near-value date, in which case there are just two elements to the transaction

- a regular exchange of interest payments over the swap period
- an exchange of principal at the far-value date (maturity).

This is illustrated in the diagram on page 9 where the currencies swapped are dollars and euros.

In practice, most swaps *do* involve an exchange of principal at the near-value date, but it is largely immaterial whether this exchange of principal actually takes place or whether it is notional.

What Happens in a Swap?

To understand how a swap works, consider the following diagram. Suppose that Counterparty A wants to take on a liability (i.e. borrow) in one currency, sterling, for a period of several years,

- paying regular interest in sterling, and
- making a principal repayment in sterling at the end of the period.

Currency Swap

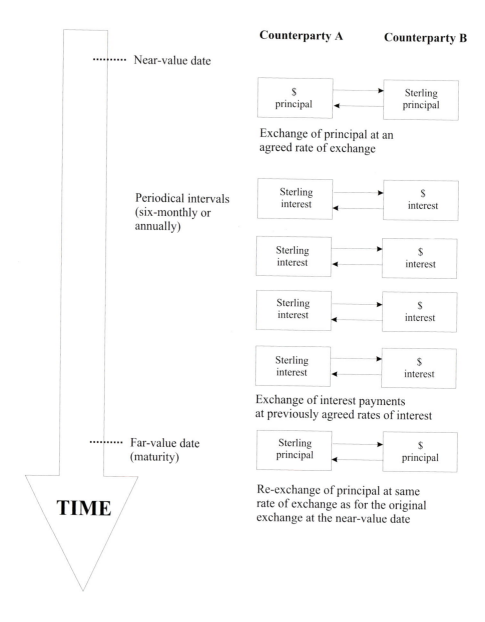

Currency Swap (with no exchange of principal at the near-value date)

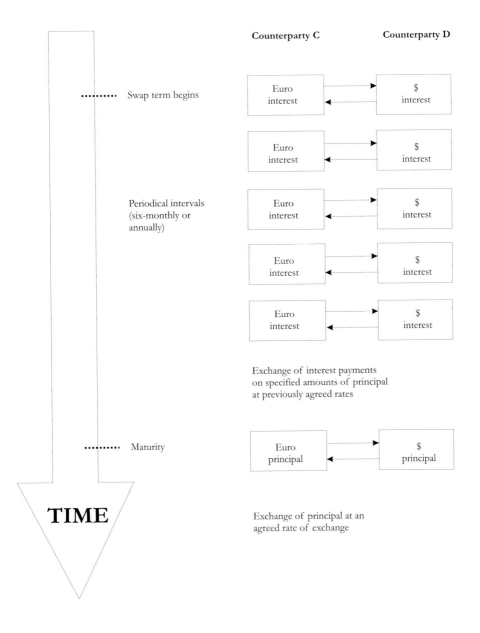

Similarly, Counterparty B wants to assume the same amount of liability but in dollars, for the same period

- paying regular interest in dollars, and
- making a principal repayment in dollars at the end of the period.

Suppose that Counterparty A wants to borrow £10 million, Counterparty B wants to borrow $15 million, and the exchange rate is $1.50 = £1.

Counterparty A could borrow £10 million in sterling and Counterparty B could borrow $15 million. Alternatively, Counterparty A can borrow $15 million dollars, Counterparty B can borrow £10 million, and they can arrange a currency swap.

Under the swap arrangement, the two parties will exchange principal at the near-value date.

- Counterparty A, having borrowed $15 million, will give the dollars to Counterparty B. Counterparty B will pay interest to Counterparty A on the $15 million, and at the swap's maturity (probably scheduled to coincide with the maturity of Counterparty A's dollar loan), Counterparty B will repay the principal ($15 million) to Counterparty A.
- Similarly, Counterparty B, having borrowed £10 million will give this to Counterparty A at the start of the swap. Counterparty A will then pay interest in sterling on this principal to Counterparty B. At the swap's maturity, Counterparty A will then pay back the £10 million to Counterparty B.

The swap thus enables each party to exchange a liability from one currency into another. Counterparty A can borrow sterling but make payments in dollars, and Counterparty B can borrow dollars, but make payments in sterling.

The rate at which the principal is exchanged in a currency swap, both at the start of the swap and at maturity, is usually the spot rate at the transaction date (i.e. when the swap is agreed between the counterparties).

Elements of a Currency Swap

There are several important elements in a currency swap that must be agreed between the two parties

- the period of the agreement
- the two currencies involved
- the principal amount of each currency, and the exchange rate
- the basis for the exchange of interest rate payments
- whether or not there will be an exchange of principal at the near-value date.

Period of the Agreement
Swaps are medium- to long-term arrangements, normally covering two to 10 years, at the end of which principal is exchanged. A five-year arrangement is probably the most common.

Currencies Involved
Most currency swaps involve the dollar and one other major currency (euro, sterling, yen, Swiss francs, Canadian dollars or Australian dollars). Swaps between two currencies other than the dollar are less common but can be arranged. As a guide to the currencies most commonly swapped, the table below gives an analysis of currency swaps outstanding as at December 31 1997. (The figures have been adjusted to allow for the fact that each currency swap involves two currencies.)

Principal Amounts
Swaps are primarily instruments for large organizations only, because the amount of currency involved in a swap is large, usually between $7

million and $150 million. Some swaps arranged in conjunction with bond issues have been for even larger amounts.

Table 1: *Currency Swaps Outstanding: December 31 1997*

Currency	$ equivalent	Percentage of total
	($ millions)	%
Dollars	351,154	30.9
Yen	136,162	12.0
Swiss francs	21,781	1.9
Deutschemarks	130,194	11.5
Australian dollars	26,530	2.3
Canadian dollars	23,664	2.1
Sterling	39,471	3.5
Ecu	17,093	1.5
Italian lira	36,856	3.2
Spanish pesetas	8,506	0.7
French francs	36,897	3.2
Swedish krona	7,021	0.6
Dutch guilders	12,243	1.2
Belgian francs	6,555	0.6
Danish krone	3,704	0.3
Hong Kong dollars	8,406	0.8
New Zealand dollars	5,652	0.5
Other currencies	263,503	23.2
	1,135,392	100.0

(Source: ISDA*)*

Interest Rate Basis

Currency swaps, strictly defined, involve an exchange of two fixed interest payment streams (i.e. a fixed-against-fixed swap). However, currency swaps also can involve

- a fixed interest rate versus a floating rate index (e.g. LIBOR)
- two floating rate indices (e.g. six month sterling LIBOR versus six month dollar LIBOR).

A currency swap in which at least one payment stream is based on a floating rate index is sometimes called a cross currency swap:

- a fixed-against-floating swap is a cross currency interest rate swap
- a floating-against-floating swap is a currency basis swap

Type of swap	Interest rate basis
Currency swap	Fixed-against-fixed
Cross currency interest rate swap	Fixed-against-floating
Currency basis swap	Floating-against-floating

Interest rates in a swap are determined by negotiation between the two parties and need not be the same as current market rates.

Interest rate payments normally are exchanged at regular intervals, six monthly or annually. The amount payable by each party must be specified in the agreement. This might be a fixed percentage (e.g. 10% annually or 5% every six months) or a floating rate (e.g. the dollar LIBOR rate for six months or 12 months).

Receiver and Payer

Each counterparty to a currency swap can be described in terms of

- the type of interest (fixed or floating), and the currency that he/she pays, and also
- the type of interest and the currency that he/she receives.

For example, in a cross currency interest rate swap, one of the counterparties might be a payer of six-month dollar LIBOR and a receiver of five year sterling fixed interest. (The other counterparty therefore will pay five-year sterling fixed interest and receive six-month dollar LIBOR.)

For most currency swaps one component is the dollar, involving the receipt (or payment) of floating dollars and the payment (or receipt) of a fixed or floating rate in the other currency; for example, an arrangement to pay 8% in sterling at six-monthly intervals in exchange for receiving interest at six-month dollar LIBOR. The reason for using dollar LIBOR is that a large proportion of cash-market funding (from banks or commercial paper markets) is based on floating dollar interest rates.

Interest Rate Exposure

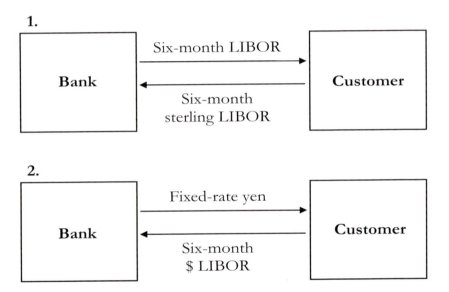

In the first agreement shown in the diagram, the customer is a payer of floating sterling against dollar LIBOR, and in the second agreement the customer is a receiver of fixed yen against dollar LIBOR.

Example
Gamma arranges a currency swap with Omega Bank of $150 million at an agreed exchange rate of $1.50 = £1, the current spot rate. Gamma agrees to sell the dollars now to Omega Bank in exchange for £100 million, and to buy them back in five years' time at $1.50 = £1. For the duration of the swap, interest rate payments will be exchanged according to the arrangement that recognizes the cost to Gamma of raising and

financing $150 million and the cost to Omega Bank of raising and financing £100 million.

The agreed interest exchange is for Gamma to pay a fixed interest rate on sterling and receive a variable interest rate on the dollar (dollar LIBOR). Gamma therefore is a payer of fixed sterling against dollar LIBOR.

The interest rate exchanges compensate each party to the swap for agreeing to re-exchange the principal amounts ($150 million and £100 million) in five years' time but at today's spot rates. These interest payments are the equivalent of premiums or discounts (i.e. the forward points) in a forward exchange contract that reflect the interest rate differential between the two currencies.

Swap Payments

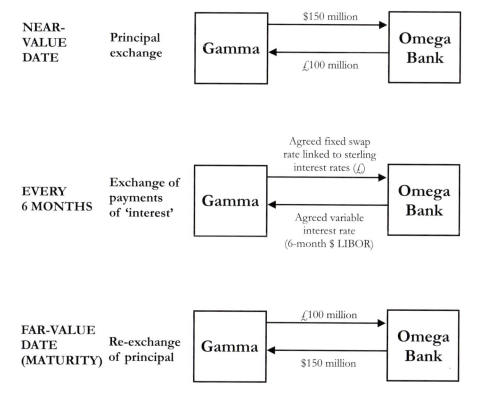

Interest Payments

It is convenient to refer to interest payments or interest exchanges on a swap, but this can be misleading. Interest is associated with a loan, but there is no loan in a swap. A swap involves an exchange of cash flows, at swap rates, based on notional amounts of principal. Technically, swaps are not loans, but rather exchanges of cash flows.

This is an important point to understand. Suppose that Alpha borrows $14 million from its US bank and Beta borrows £10 million from its UK bank, and they arrange a swap for these amounts (at an agreed exchange rate of $1.40 = £1). Under the swap agreement Alpha will make regular sterling payments to Beta, in exchange for payments by Beta in dollars.

Principal Swap, Near-value Date

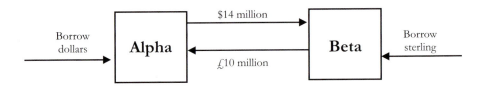

Exchanges of 'interest' payments

The swap arrangement allows Alpha to become a payer of sterling and Beta to become a payer of dollars.

	Alpha	**Beta**
Loan	- Pay dollars	- Pay sterling
Swap	+ Receive dollars	+ Receive sterling
Swap	- Pay sterling	- Pay dollars
Net result	- Pay sterling	- Pay dollars

In spite of the swap, however, Alpha remains liable for the dollar loan to its bank and Beta is liable for its sterling loan. The loan commitments of the two counterparties have not been exchanged. If, for example, Alpha defaulted on the swap and refused to continue to make payments to Beta, Beta would be left with its liabilities in sterling, making sterling interest payments to its bank and eventually having to repay the loan on maturity, without the sterling inflows from Alpha to cover these payments.

Example
A German and a US multinational company both want to raise funds. The German company, Bundes AG, wants to borrow dollars for five-years and the US company, Federal Inc., wants to borrow euros for a similar period. Current yields on five-year loans would be 5% on euros for the German company and 4% on dollars for the US company. The German company could borrow dollars but would have to pay a higher rate than 4% per annum (perhaps because it is an unknown foreign borrower in the US financial markets). Similarly, the US company could borrow euros but would have to pay slightly more than 5% per annum. We shall assume that the loan principal in each case will be repaid in full (as a bullet repayment) at the end of the loan term.

The current euro/dollar exchange rate is €1 = $1.20.

Analysis
Under a swap agreement, a bank would match the needs of the two companies, acting as intermediary. (In this example, we shall ignore the bank's profit margin on the swap.) There would have to be agreement on

● the amount of principal to swap

- the exchange rate
- the period of the agreement
- interest rates payable
- the frequency of exchange of interest.

The exchange rate selected is the current rate of €1 = $1.20, and the amounts of the swap are €10 million and $12 million.

Bundes AG would borrow €10 million at 5% per annum for five years in the capital markets, and Federal Inc. would borrow $12 million for five years at 4%, with interest payable six-monthly in both cases. Under a swap agreement, the two companies could agree to exchange these amounts of principal at the near-value date, so that Bundes AG obtains dollars and Federal Inc. obtains euros. Alternatively, each company simply could sell the currency it has borrowed in exchange for the currency it wants, i.e. Bundes AG could borrow €10 million and sell them for dollars (at €1 = $1.20) in the foreign exchange market. Similarly Federal Inc could borrow $12 million and sell them in exchange for euros in the FX market.

Interest would be swapped every six months to coincide with the underlying loan obligations of both companies. Bundes AG would pay dollar interest to Federal Inc. at 8% per annum and Federal Inc. would pay Euro interest to Bundes AG at 4% per annum.

At the end of five years, there will be a final interest exchange and a re-exchange of principal. Bundes AG would pay $12 million to Federal Inc., that would in return pay back €10 million. Both companies could then use the principal to repay their underlying loan obligations.

By means of this swap arrangement, the original purpose has been achieved. Bundes AG has obtained a five-year dollar liability and Federal Inc. a five-year euro liability, although their actual loans were in euros and dollars respectively.

		Bundes AG	**Federal Inc**
		Borrow €10 million	Borrow $12 million
		Swap liability into dollars	Swap liability into euros
Interest payments on loan		- Euros at 5%	- Dollars at 4%
Swap payments			
	Receive	+ Euros 5%	+ Dollars at 4%
	Pay	- Dollars at 4%	- Euros at 5%
Net result:	Pay	- Dollars at 4%	- Euros at 5%
End of swap			
Exchange of principal	Pay	- $12 million	- €10 million
	Receive	+ €10 million	+ $12 million
Actual loan repayment	Pay	- €10 million	- $12 million
Net result	Pay	- $12 million	- €10 million

Exchanges of interest in a currency swap normally involve a payment in one currency and a receipt in the other currency. In some swap transactions, however, the counterparties agree to net the opposite payments, so that on each interest payment date, there is a single payment from one counterparty to the other. To net the interest payments, the cash flow in one currency has to be translated into the other, usually dollars.

For example, suppose that a currency swap involves the exchange of $20 million for €17 million, with interest payable annually at 4% on the dollars and 5% on the euros. The annual exchange of interest will call for the payment of $800,000 in return for €850,000. A net payment could be agreed, whereby the payment in euros is translated into dollars at the spot rate for example. If the spot rate for one payment is € = $1.20, the payment in euros would translate into $1,020,000 (€850,000 x 1.20). The counterparty receiving dollars and paying euros would make a net payment of $220,000.

Comparison With Forward Contracts

A forward exchange contract involves an agreement now for the sale or purchase of a quantity of one currency in exchange for another currency at a specified future date. The rate of exchange is the spot rate adjusted for the interest rate differential between the two currencies over the period of the forward contract.

For example, suppose that the current sterling/dollar exchange rate is $2 = £1 and that the interest rate on the dollar and sterling is 4% and 8% per annum respectively. Although £1,000 has the same value now as $2,000, by investing these equivalent amounts of money, £1,000 invested for one year at 8% would be worth £1,080 and $2,000 invested for one year at 4% would be worth $2,080. A one-year forward contract for the dollar against sterling would have an exchange rate that reflected the interest rate differential between the two currencies, as follows

One year forward rate = $2 x 1.04/1.08 = $1.9259 to £1

The interest rate on the dollar is lower, therefore the dollar will be quoted forward at a more expensive rate against sterling than the current spot rate. This is the same as saying that although $2,000 has the same value as £1,000 now ($2 = £1 spot), after one year $2,080 is equivalent to £1,080 and so $1.9259 = £1 (2,080 ÷ 1,080). Therefore a one-year forward contract could be arranged to sell $2,080 in exchange for £1,080, i.e. the dollar could be sold at a forward rate of $1.9259.

This forward contract would be the same as a one-year currency swap where there is no exchange of principal at the near-value date, and no exchange of interest payments until the end of the swap period. A one-year swap arrangement between two counterparties might be based on notional amounts of £1,000 and $2,000 ($2 = £1), with

- no exchange of principal at the near-value date
- exchange of interest at the end of one year, with interest on the dollar at 4% and on sterling at 8%

- exchange of $2,000 for £1,000 (today's spot rate) at the far-value date (after one year).

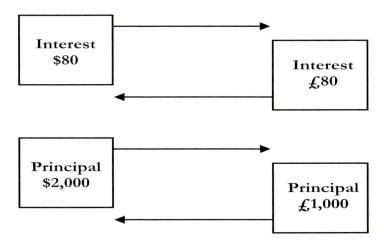

The exchange of cash after one year is $2,080 for £1,080, exactly the same as with a forward contract.

However, currency swaps differ from outright forward contracts, because

- there is often an exchange of principal at the near-value date
- the period of a swap is longer than for most forward contracts
- interest usually is exchanged at regular intervals during the swap period (an exception is the zero-coupon swap that is described later)
- the regular exchange of interest means that the (re-)exchange of principal at the far-value date can be at today's spot rate, i.e. the spot rate at the start of the swap period.

Therefore a currency swap can be used as a surrogate long-term forward contract, and could be particularly useful for hedging currency exposures when a forward contract cannot be obtained.

Currency Swaps and Forward Swaps

There is an even closer similarity between

- forward swaps, and
- currency swaps where the swap involves an exchange of principal at the near-value date as well as at maturity.

A forward swap in the FX markets is

- a spot purchase of a quantity of currency and a simultaneous forward sale of the same amount, or
- a spot sale of a quantity of currency and a simultaneous forward purchase of the same amount.

An example of a forward swap would be whereby a company arranges to sell $480,000 to a bank on June 1 in exchange for sterling at a rate of $1.5000, and simultaneously agrees to buy $480,000 from the bank on August 1 at a rate of $1.4950 for example. This type of swap transaction (also called a sell and buy transaction) is used when a company asks its bank to extend the settlement date of an existing forward contract. Forward swaps between banks are very common.

The difference between the spot price and the forward price depends on the interest rate differential between the two currencies.

Suppose, for example, that the current sterling/dollar exchange rate is $1.50 = £1, and that one-year interest rates are 4% on the dollar and 7% on sterling. The one-year forward rate for the dollar against sterling could be calculated as follows

	Sterling	Dollars
Spot	100	150
Interest for one year	7	6
	107	156

One-year forward rate $156/£107 = $1.4579 to £1

(*Note*: The forward rate is derived from the interest rate differential between the dollar and sterling.)

Suppose now that a one-year dollar/sterling currency swap could be arranged in which the principal amounts are exchanged at the near-value date, and interest payments are exchanged at the rate of 4% per annum for the dollar and 7% for sterling.

A comparison of the forward swap and the currency swap, for £10 million in sterling and $15 million, would be as follows.

Currency Swaps and Forward Swaps Compared

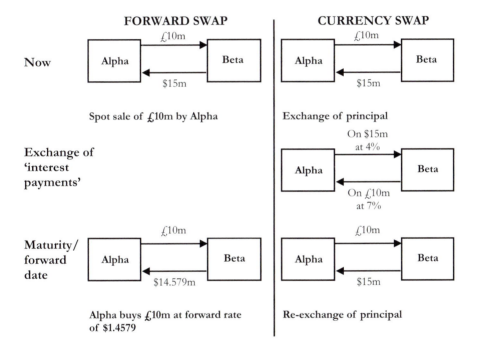

The re-exchange of principal in the currency swap is at the original spot rate because the interest rate differential between sterling and the dollar is reflected in the payments of swap interest.

The currency swap and the FX market forward swap are similar in that they both involve the exchange and subsequent re-exchange of currencies. However, some differences do exist.

- In a currency swap, the initial exchange and subsequent re-exchange of principal are at the same rate of exchange. With a forward swap, there is a difference in the exchange rate between the initial exchange and the subsequent re-exchange. As with all forward contracts, the rate for the later exchange of currency is at a premium or discount to the spot rate that reflects the interest rate differential between the two currencies over the time period.
- Normally a currency swap has a term of at least two years, and there are (normally) regular exchanges of interest during its term. Forward swaps are not long term, and there is no exchange of interest.

Origins of Currency Swaps

Currency swaps originally were developed by banks in the UK to help large clients circumvent UK exchange controls in the 1970s. UK companies, seeking to finance their US subsidiaries' operations, were required to pay a premium (known as an exchange equalization premium or the investment premium) when obtaining dollar loans from their banks. The idea behind a swap was to avoid having to pay this premium for dollar borrowing. A bank would identify a UK-based organization that wanted to borrow in dollars and a US-based organization wanting a sterling loan. An agreement would then be negotiated whereby

- the UK organization borrowed sterling and lent it to the US company's UK subsidiary
- the US organization borrowed dollars and lent it to the UK company's US subsidiary.

The UK organization would take on the obligation to pay dollar interest and repay the dollar loan principal, and the US organization similarly would take on the liability to pay sterling interest and repay the sterling loan principal.

No sterling left the UK and no dollars left the US, so there was no requirement to pay the exchange equalization premium on dollars. The benefit of cheaper borrowing could be shared between both parties to the swap, and both the US and UK organizations therefore could pay less for currency debt liabilities than if they had borrowed directly in the foreign currency (sterling or dollars).

These early arrangements were called *back-to-back loans* or *parallel loans*, from which more sophisticated currency swaps were gradually developed over time.

One of the earliest and most widely reported currency swaps was arranged in August 1981, with Salomon Brothers acting as intermediary between IBM and the World Bank.

IBM had existing debts in deutschemarks and Swiss francs. Because of a depreciation of the deutschemark and Swiss franc against the dollar, IBM could realize a large foreign exchange gain on its currency borrowings, but only if it could eliminate its deutschemark and Swiss franc liabilities and "lock in" the gain, i.e. remove the risk that exchange rates could move the other way, and thereby erode the profit.

The World Bank at that time was raising most of its funds in deutschemarks and Swiss francs, on which interest rates were about 12% and 8% respectively. It did not borrow in dollars, for which the interest cost was about 17%. Although it wanted to lend to its borrowers in deutschemarks and Swiss francs, the bank was concerned that saturation in the bond markets, especially for Swiss francs, could make it difficult to borrow more in those currencies at a suitable rate of interest.

The currency swap proposed by Salomon Brothers satisfied the requirements of both counterparties. IBM could realize a profit on its currency borrowings, and was willing to take on dollar liabilities, despite the high interest rate. The World Bank could borrow dollars, convert them into deutschemarks and Swiss francs, and through the swap take on payment obligations in deutschemarks and Swiss francs.

World Bank/IBM Currency Swap, 1981

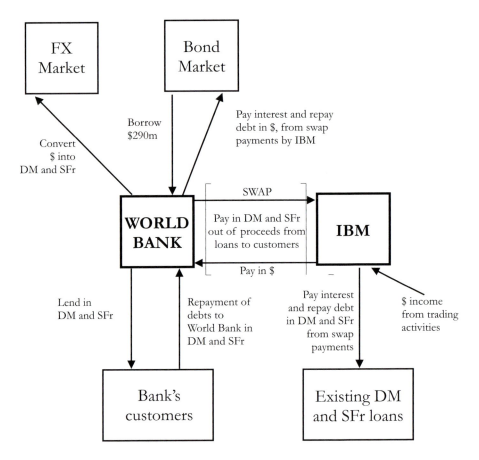

Notes

1. The swap payments by the World Bank to IBM were scheduled so as to allow IBM to meet its debt repayment obligations in DM and SFr.
2. IBM and the World Bank at the time had triple-A credit ratings; therefore the counterparty credit risk in the swap was low.

Conclusion

Swaps are not a method of borrowing money, but rather a means of managing debt and funding requirements. Primarily they are used to

- create cheaper funds/debt: a swap can reduce the overall cost of borrowing (liability swap)
- improve income from investments (asset swap)
- hedge longer-term currency exposures and reduce an organization's financial risk.

Currency swaps in effect are long-term forward contracts for foreign exchange (an FX forward).

A currency swap is also classified as a derivative instrument although, strictly speaking, it is not a derivative. A derivative is an instrument whose performance is derived from the price of an underlying commodity in a cash market (e.g. a quantity of currency in the foreign exchange market or eurocurrency market), but that does not require that the underlying commodity actually should be bought or sold. A currency swap is not, strictly speaking, a derivative because there is a requirement for the eventual exchange of a principal amount in one currency for a principal amount in a second currency at the end of the swap agreement.

The Role of Banks

Swaps are arranged between two banks or between a bank and a company or institution. Banks employ specialist teams whose task is to identify large companies or other institutions that might be interested in a swap transaction, and subsequently to negotiate terms with them.

Financial Risks

A bank that acts as counterparty in a currency swap has three types of financial risk to consider

- credit risk
- interest rate risk
- currency risk.

Measures always can be taken to hedge the interest rate risk and the currency risk.

Credit risk arises because the counterparty to the swap could fail to make a payment. Interest rate risk arises from the possibility that after a swap has been transacted, market interest rates could move against one of the counterparties, and in favor of the other (so that one counterparty is paying an interest rate in the swap that is higher than the current market rate, or is receiving an interest rate that is lower).

Currency risk arises from the possibility that the exchange rate will alter, so that the exchange of interest and principal in the swap will benefit one counterparty to the disadvantage of the other.

The various types of financial risk in a currency swap can be illustrated with the example below.

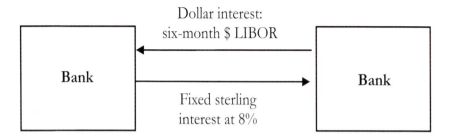

Dollar interest:
six-month $ LIBOR

Bank

Bank

Fixed sterling
interest at 8%

A bank transacts a swap with a customer in which the bank pays fixed interest in sterling at 8% and receives dollar interest at a floating rate. There will be an exchange of principal (£10 million for $14 million) at the maturity of the swap in three years' time.

Analysis
Unless the bank takes hedging measures, it will be exposed to credit risk, interest rate risk and currency risk.

To limit the risk that the customer will default on a payment, the bank will not agree to transact the swap without first carrying out a credit assessment of the customer.

The interest rate risk arises from the possibility that, after the swap has been transacted

- dollar LIBOR will fall, and the interest receivable from the swap therefore will fall, or
- sterling interest rates will fall, so that the bank will be paying fixed interest in the swap at above the current market rate.

The currency risk for the bank arises from the possibility that the dollar will weaken in value more than expected. The exchange of principal at maturity is based on an exchange rate of $1.40 = £1. At a rate of $1.60 = £1, for example, the bank would have to pay £10 million to the customer at maturity, but the value of the $14 million receivable would be less than originally anticipated when the swap was transacted.

Matched Transactions

Swaps can be arranged to suit the specific requirements of a particular client. A bank would then find matching counterparties who want to arrange an exact or near exact opposite swap. For example, if Alpha wishes to pay fixed sterling in exchange for dollar LIBOR, and Beta wishes to receive fixed sterling in exchange for dollar LIBOR, for the same amount of principal, a bank can execute two simultaneous swap transactions. In doing so, it would avoid being exposed to any currency or interest rate risk.

Example
Cobra Bank arranges a five-year $200 million swap with the Theta Company in which the company is a receiver of fixed sterling at 6.25% against dollar LIBOR.

Concurrently, Cobra Bank arranges a five-year $200 million swap with a government institution in which the institution is a payer of fixed sterling at 6.50% against dollar LIBOR.

Interest Rate Flows (Semi-Annual)

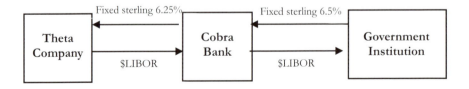

Cobra Bank's profit comes from the interest rate differential between the rate at which the bank will receive and pay fixed interest on sterling, in this case 0.25% per annum for the life of the swap.

In the early years of the swaps market, banks tried to match transactions but it is difficult to match the requirements of two clients simultaneously. With the evolution and development of the market, however, banks now usually arrange a swap for one customer without structuring a simultaneous and matching swap with another counterparty.

Instead of acting as an intermediary to arrange a swap transaction between Client A and Client B, the swaps bank will itself act as counterparty in each of the two swaps.

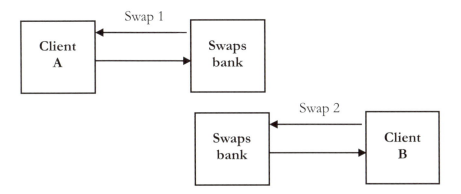

The two legs of the arrangement will be made at different times, and in the period between making the two matching swap agreements, the bank will have an exposure to interest rate and currency risk.

Profiting from Trading

Profits from swaps trading come from the differential between the rates at which currency interest is received under some swap agreements and paid under others. Swaps banks usually do not charge arrangement fees or commissions. In some countries this is because companies cannot deduct swap arrangement fees for tax purposes. Consequently, banks consider arrangement costs when setting their swap rates.

Because arrangement costs are roughly the same for swaps of any size, building the cost into swap rates means that the spread will be much wider for swaps with a smaller principal value than for higher value swaps.

Occasionally, a bank might intermediate on large swaps, acting as counterparty between another swaps bank and a customer, and lending its name to the arrangement.

In doing so, it takes on both sides of the credit risk in the swap, and will earn a margin of a few basis points, say 0.05% of the principal amount.

Example
Alpha Bank's swaps team has identified two clients who would like to arrange a five-year swap agreement.

- Client X is about to issue £10 million of sterling bonds at 8%, with interest payable half-yearly. It would like to swap this sterling liability into a floating-rate dollar liability.
- Client Y is paying variable rate interest on a loan of $15 million. Interest is based on six-month dollar LIBOR and the loan has a further five years to maturity. Client Y would like to swap this dollar liability for a fixed-rate sterling liability.

The current spot rate is $1.50 = £1.

Swap with Client X
Initial exchange of principal

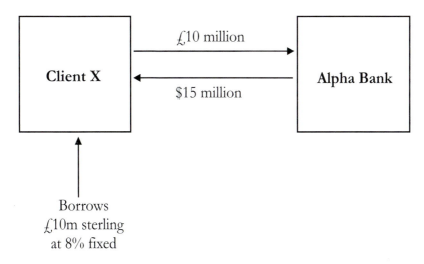

Interest exchange (six-monthly)

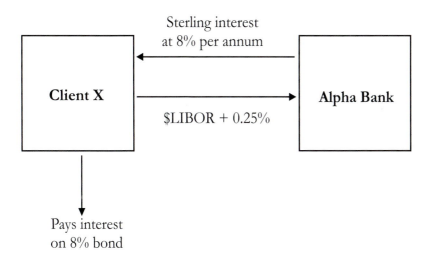

Re-exchange of principal at far-value date (after five years)

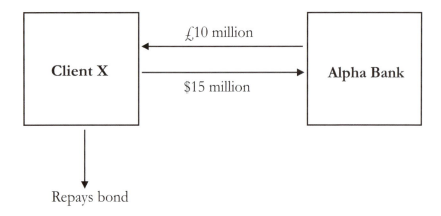

Analysis

Alpha Bank could arrange two separate swap agreements, at roughly the same time. The terms would be subject to negotiation but might be as follows.

Swap 1. In a five-year swap between Alpha Bank and Client X, Client X would be a receiver of sterling against dollar LIBOR. The initial exchange of principal would be £10 million for $15 million (at the spot rate of $1.50).

Interest payments would be every six months, with Client X receiving 8% fixed sterling and paying six-month dollar LIBOR plus 0.25%. This swap is shown on page 35.

Swap 2. In a five-year swap between Client Y and Alpha Bank, Client Y will be a payer of fixed sterling against dollar LIBOR. Interest payable every six months would be at 8.25% per annum in sterling, against receipt of dollar interest at six month dollar LIBOR. This swap is shown on page 37.

The bank, acting as intermediary between two clients, has no currency exposure of its own, and makes a profit on interest rate margins.

In this example, the net revenue for the bank is 0.25% on £10 million (8.25% - 8%), plus 0.25% per annum on $15 million.

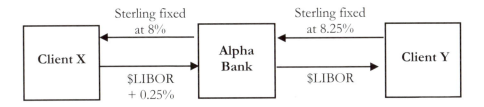

Multi-Legged Swaps

In a multi-legged swap a bank avoids taking on any currency risk itself by arranging three or more swaps with different clients in order to match currencies and amounts. For example, suppose Alpha Bank has three swaps clients P, Q and R

- Client P wants to be a receiver of fixed yen against dollar LIBOR
- Client Q wants to be a receiver of fixed sterling against fixed yen
- Client R wants to be a payer of fixed sterling against dollar LIBOR.

Swap with client Y
Initial exchange of principal

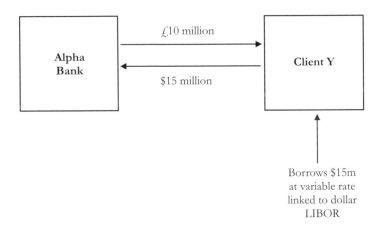

Interest exchange (six-monthly)

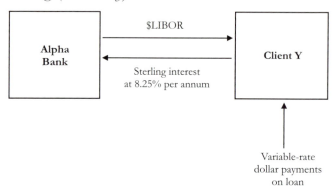

Re-exchange of principal at far-value date (after five years)

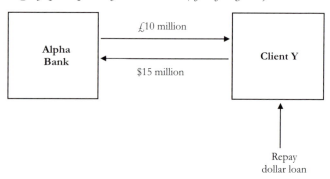

The requirements of all three clients could be met by a three-legged swap, and provided the amount of currency and the period of the swap satisfies each client's requirements, the arrangement would be as follows

Multi-Legged Swap

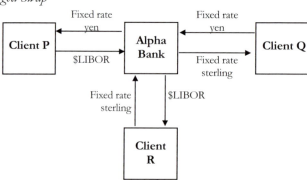

It can be difficult to swap directly between some currencies, particularly where floating rate payments are required in a non-dollar currency. In these cases, a swap bank can arrange a multi-legged structure to meet the customer's requirements.

Example

A company wishes to arrange a swap in which it receives floating rate interest on Australian dollars and pays fixed interest on sterling. A swap bank agrees to the transaction, and arranges a multi-legged structure involving three swaps

- a fixed sterling versus floating Australian dollar swap with the company
- a floating Australian dollar versus floating dollar swap with another counterparty, Counterparty A
- a fixed sterling versus floating dollar swap with another counterparty, Counterparty B.

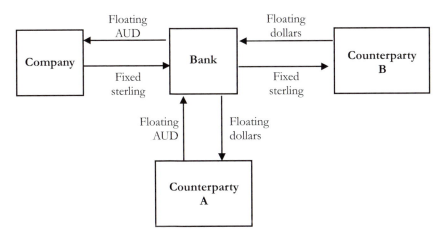

Swaps Book

Because swaps are tailored to customer requirements, it is difficult to match in full the requirements of every customer, even in a multi-legged swap. The swaps bank is most likely to take on some of the swaps obligations, and therefore the risk, into its own book. Specialist swaps banks, by building up a portfolio of swap commitments, will try to manage and limit the risks from its unmatched swaps.

Basis Swaps

Basis swaps commonly are used by banks to construct a currency swap for a customer. The customer might want to pay or receive fixed interest in one (or both) of the currencies. Even so, the bank uses a basis swap to arrange the transaction.

Suppose for example that a customer wants to arrange a swap in which he/she pays fixed dollars and receives fixed sterling. The customer's requirement can be met, but to do so, the bank might arrange three other separate swap transactions, as follows

- an interest rate swap, fixed rate against floating rate, in dollars
- a currency basis swap, floating dollars against floating sterling
- an interest rate swap, fixed sterling against floating sterling.

The combined result is shown below

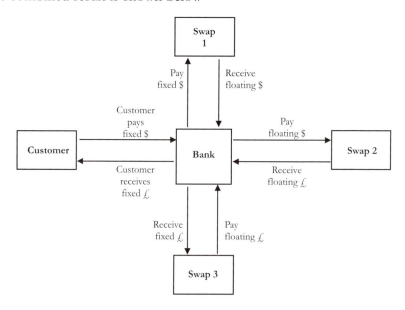

The three swap transactions, two interest rate swaps and one currency basis swap, allow the bank to set up the fixed sterling/fixed dollar swap for the customer.

Similarly, if a customer wishes to swap floating rate euros in exchange for fixed rate dollars, the swaps bank could arrange two underlying swap agreements

- a fixed dollars against floating dollars interest rate swap
- a floating rate dollars against floating rate euros currency basis swap.

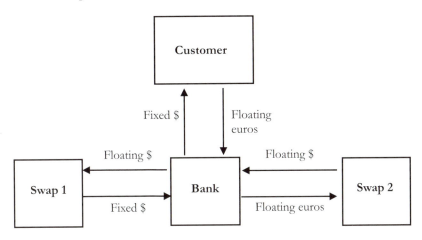

Hedging the Bank's Risk

Exposures inevitably arise for a swaps bank from mismatched principal amounts, currencies, and maturities. The bank therefore will assume some currency and interest rate risk that it could try to hedge in the government bond market.

- If the bank is paying a fixed rate on a swap, it could buy government bonds as a hedge.
- If the bank is receiving a fixed rate on a swap, it could sell

government bonds as a hedge.
- If the bank is paying or receiving a variable rate (e.g. dollar LIBOR) it can hedge its position by lending or borrowing in the money markets.

When the bank finds a counterparty to transact a matching swap in the other direction, it will liquidate its hedge, reversing the original sale or purchase of bonds.

Example

A swaps bank arranges a swap with Client Z in which the client is a receiver of fixed sterling against dollar LIBOR. There is no matching swap yet available in the other direction, and the bank decides to hedge its interest rate and currency exposure in the bond market.

Analysis

The bank will be paying fixed sterling, and so will buy gilts (UK government securities) to hedge its exposure. The sterling interest it receives from the gilts can be offset against the sterling paid under the swap exchanges of interest. The bank could buy enough gilts so that the income matches the swap payments exactly.

The Key Banks

In the US and Europe several banks specialize in currency swaps. They include the major commercial banks such as Deutsche Bank and Société Générale as well as several investment banks including J P Morgan, Goldman Sachs, Morgan Stanley, Merrill Lynch and CS First Boston.

4

Types of Currency Swap

Currency swaps can be of different types, according to their terms and conditions. They include

- plain vanilla or generic swaps
- amortizing swaps
- zero coupon swaps
- differential swaps.

Plain Vanilla Currency Swaps (Generic Swaps)

The term plain vanilla is more commonly applied to interest rate swaps than currency swaps. A swap is plain vanilla or generic if it has standard terms and no modifications. For a currency swap to be plain vanilla

- there must be an exchange of principal at the near-value date as well as a re-exchange at the far-value date
- the agreed rate of exchange must be the current spot rate
- the swap period should commence two days from the agreement being made because spot transactions in the FX markets are settled after two working days
- there should be an exchange of fixed-against-floating interest
- the second currency is swapped (at a constant fixed rate of interest) against six-month dollar LIBOR with annual interest payments in the case of euros and Swiss francs and semi-annual payments in the case of the yen and sterling

- there must be no special risk features in the terms of the swap agreement.

Amortizing Swaps

Amortizing swaps require that the principal amount is reduced progressively by a series of re-exchanges during the life of the swap to match the amortization schedule of the underlying transaction (typical in asset-backed finance using swaps, such as aircraft, plant or shipping transactions).

Example 1
A company has an outstanding dollar loan that is being paid off gradually over three years. The company would like to swap this dollar liability into a sterling liability.

Under an amortizing swap agreement, there could be

- an exchange of principal at the near-value date; the company receiving dollars in exchange for sterling
- an annual re-exchange of part of the principal amount; the company receiving sufficient dollars each year to meet the repayment schedule on its loan
- regular exchanges of interest; the company paying fixed sterling against dollar LIBOR and the amount of interest being reduced with the gradual re-exchange of principal.

Example 2
Romeo Inc has a dollar loan of $24 million, on which the principal is repayable in equal amounts of $6 million over the next four years. Interest is payable annually at dollar LIBOR plus ½%. The company would like to swap its dollar liability into a sterling liability. The current spot rate is $1.60 = £1. Victor Bank is willing to arrange an amortizing swap with annual exchanges of payments, and with Romeo Inc being a

payer of fixed sterling at 10% against dollar LIBOR plus ½%. There would be no exchange of principal at the near-value date. Romeo's dollar receipts under the swap agreement will match the payments under its dollar loan agreement.

Analysis

Romeo Inc will receive dollar payments under the swap arrangements sufficient to pay the interest and repay the loan principal on its dollar loan. In exchange, Romeo will pay interest and principal in sterling to Victor Bank.

The exchange of payments, both principal and interest, would be as follows

Exchange of Principal

End of	Currency	Romeo plc		Victor Bank	
		Pays	Receives	Pays	Receives
		£ million	$ million	$ million	£ million
Year 1	dollars		6	6	
	sterling	3.75			3.75
Year 2	dollars		6	6	
	sterling	3.75			3.75
Year 3	dollars		6	6	
	sterling	3.75			3.75
Year 4	dollars		6	6	
	sterling	3.75			3.75

Exchange of Interest (Annual)

End of	Currency	Romeo plc Pays	Romeo plc Receives	Victor Bank Pays	Victor Bank Receives
		£ million	$ million	$ million	£ million
Year 1	dollars				
	(on $24 million)		LIBOR + ½%	LIBOR + ½%	
	sterling				
	(on £15 million)	1.500			1.500
Year 2	dollars				
	(on $18 million)		LIBOR + ½%	LIBOR + ½%	
	sterling				
	(on £11.25 million)	1.125			1.125
Year 3	dollars				
	(on $12 million)		LIBOR + ½%	LIBOR + ½%	
	sterling				
	(on £7.5 million)	0.750			0.750
Year 4	dollars				
	(on $6 million)		LIBOR + ½%	LIBOR + ½%	
	sterling				
	(on £3.75 million)	0.375			0.375

Zero Coupon Swaps

With zero coupon swaps there is no interim exchange of interest. The interest differential is rolled up into the final re-exchange rate that consequently is different from the rate applied to the initial exchange by the amount of accumulated interest. This is the swap structure that is the closest substitute for forward foreign exchange transactions.

Example
Assume that a company wishes to sell $6.7 million six years' forward to

hedge anticipated dollar income. The following price assumptions would apply to the swap

The current spot rate is $1.50 = £1. This is selected as the rate for the exchange of principal at maturity. (There will not be an exchange of principal at the near-value date, only a notional exchange.)

Five-year interest rates are

On the dollar:	5% per annum
On sterling:	7% per annum.

Analysis
The company wants to sell $6.7 million in six years' time, and it can do this by arranging to make a payment in dollars in exchange for sterling, at the end of Year 6, under a zero coupon swap arrangement. The notional principal in the swap should be $6.7 million *discounted* to allow for the interest payments in dollars that will accumulate over the term of the swap. Because the dollar interest rate is 5%, the notional principal in the six-year swap should be $5 million; $6.7 million $\div$ $(1.05)^6$. There is no requirement for an initial exchange of principal at the near-value date. At maturity, however, the company will pay $5 million to its swap counterparty (a bank) and receive £3.33 million that is the sterling equivalent of $5 million at an exchange rate of $1.50 = £1.

The interest payment by the company will be the compound interest on a $5 million loan at 5% for six years. This is $1.7 million, bringing the full payment by the company under the swap agreement to $6.7 million ($5 million + $1.7 million). The interest payment by the swap bank will be the compound interest on £3.33 million at 7% for six years; £1.67. The flows by structuring a surrogate forward sale via currency swaps therefore will be as follows

	Bank		UK company	
	Payments	**Receipts**	**Payments**	**Receipts**
Year 6 (far-value date)	£ million	$ million	$ million	£ million
Interest flows settled				
in one transaction at				
maturity	1.67	1.70	1.70	1.67
Re-exchange of principal	3.33	5.00	5.00	3.33
Net settlement of				
swap at maturity	5.00	6.70	6.70	5.00

Notes

The exchange of principal at maturity is at the spot rate of $1.50 = £1. There are no regular exchanges of interest payments during the term of the swap, only a single payment at the end of the sixth year. These interest payments of £1.67 million in exchange for $1.70 million are calculated as follows from the fixed rates in the swap agreement.

- For sterling: [£3.3m x $(1.07)^6$] - £3.33m = £1.67m approx.
- For US dollars: [$5m x $(1.05)^6$] - $5m = $1.7m approx.

As a result of the swap, the UK company has secured an effective six-year forward rate for the $6.7 million, by receiving a guaranteed £5 million. The currency exposure has been hedged, and the effective six-year forward rate obtained is approximately $1.34 = £1 ($6.7 million ÷ $5 million).

Differential Swaps

Differential swaps, also called diff swaps or quanto swaps, are a special type of floating-against-floating currency swap that does not involve any exchange of principal, not even at maturity.

- The notional principal amount is in just one currency.
- Interest payments are exchanged by reference to a floating rate index in one currency and a floating rate index in a second

currency. Both interest rates are applied to the same notional principal.

● Interest payments are made in the same currency as the notional principal amount.

Example

Omega Bank and Zeta Bank make a dollar/euro differential swap transaction. The notional principal sum is $30 million. Omega Bank will pay interest at six-month Eurolibor and will receive at six-month dollar LIBOR. The interest streams will be paid in dollars.

Analysis

Suppose that for one of the interest payments in the swap, six-month Eurolibor is 5.8% and six-month dollar LIBOR is 4.2%. The interest period is, for example, 183 days.

	$
Omega Bank will pay 5.8% x $30 million x 183/360	884,500
and will receive 4.2% x $30 million x 183/360	640,500
Net payment to Zeta Bank	244,000

In a differential swap, both counterparties are exposed to adverse changes in the differential between the interest rates in the two currencies (hence the name given to this type of swap). For at least one of the counterparties, there need be no currency risk at all. In the example above, Zeta Bank is paying and receiving interest in dollars, based on a notional principal amount in dollars, and is unlikely to have any currency exposure to the euro/dollar exchange rate.

Diff Swaps and Currency Risk

Differential swaps commonly have been presented by banks to their clients as a method of converting their borrowings into cheap floating rate funds in currencies that normally would attract a high coupon.

A differential swap works best when the interest rates in one currency are expected to rise, and in the other are expected to fall. It is interesting to look back at a situation that applied during much of 1992-1993 when there was a sharply inverted yield curve in deutschemarks and a super-normal yield curve in dollars. The market was suggesting that the high short-term German interest rates would fall over time, while the low short-term dollar rates were expected to increase rapidly.

At the same time, there was a large interest rate differential between the dollar and the deutschemark. At one time, an investor could earn over 500 basis points (5%) more from investing in deutschemarks than from investing in dollars.

The differential swap in such circumstances allowed clients to structure borrowings in deutschemarks but pay an interest rate related to the dollar yield curve, *without taking currency risk*.

At that time, diff swaps also could be attractive to US money managers as a means of earning high DM-related interest yields related to another currency, without exposure to exchange rate risk.

During early 1999, there was an inverted yield curve in sterling and a normal yield curve in dollars, so a similar situation applied. In such a situation, a money manager, receiving dollar interest from a portfolio of US investments, could arrange a diff swap

- paying dollar LIBOR with payments in dollars, and
- receiving sterling LIBOR minus a few basis points with receipts in dollars.

A bank arranging a diff swap also would arrange two supporting interest rate swaps

- a swap in which it paid out interest at dollar LIBOR in return for fixed interest dollar income (the fixed dollar receipts would be converted into fixed sterling through the FX market)
- a swap in which it received floating rate sterling interest and paid fixed rate sterling.

Example

We can examine a diff swap based around the following interest rates, with a spot sterling/dollar rate of 1.5000.

	Dollars	**Sterling**
3 months LIBOR	3%	9%
5 years fixed	8%	7%

A client of Omega Bank has existing borrowings in sterling, paying floating-rate interest linked to sterling LIBOR. The client would like to pay the lower interest rate available on the dollar, but does not want currency exposure to the dollar.

Analysis

The client's requirements can be met by a differential swap. For a notional principal of, for example, £100 million, a differential swap structure from the client's viewpoint would be as follows

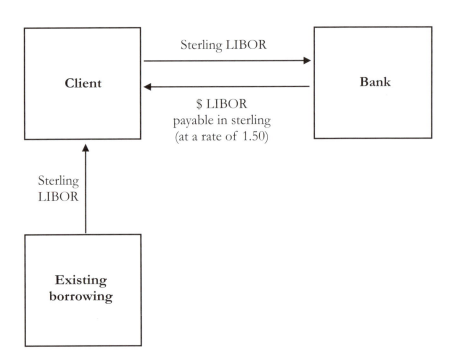

From the bank's viewpoint the structure would be as follows

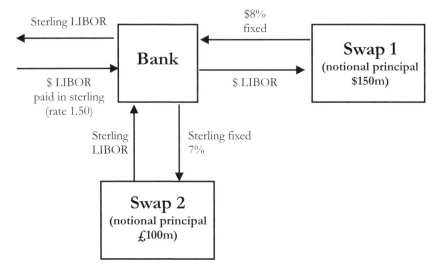

The bank is exposed to changes in the dollar/sterling exchange rate, but can take measures to hedge its position.

5

Asset Swaps

Currency swaps that investors use to alter the currency and cash flow characteristics of investment income are called asset swaps. In terms of the volume of transactions, asset swaps are far less common than liability swaps.

An asset swap might be used by an investing company such as a bank or insurance company that has investment earnings in one currency that it wishes to swap into another, without selling the underlying investment.

Example
An investment company owns £10 million of UK government securities receiving a fixed coupon rate of interest of 8%. The securities will mature in six years' time. It wishes to convert this income into floating rate dollars because it expects US interest rates to rise and the value of the dollar to strengthen.

Analysis
By arranging a currency swap, the investment company can convert its sterling cash inflows into dollar inflows at today's rates for the remaining life of the securities.

We will assume that when the swap is arranged

- the spot rate of exchange is $2 = £1
- the bank quotes a dollar/sterling swap price of 10% for receiving fixed sterling and paying dollar LIBOR.

The term of the swap will be six years, to coincide with the redemption date of the government securities.

Investing Company's Swap

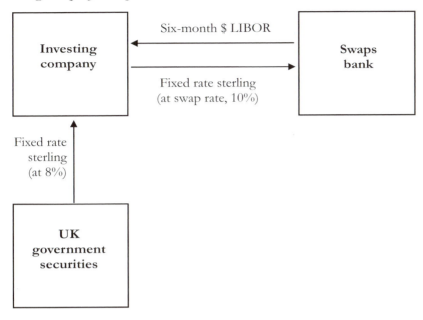

The investment company is earning a fixed £800,000 per annum in interest on its £10 million of securities, and it wishes to convert this income stream into floating rate dollars.

The swaps bank will want to receive fixed sterling at 10% against floating rate dollars. The amount of principal to provide interest of £800,000 per annum is £8 million (800,000 ÷ 10%), although the investment securities have a nominal value of £10 million and a different market value.

The terms of the swap therefore might be as follows

- At the near-value date there is no exchange of actual funds, but a nominal exchange of £8 million for $16 million (at $2 = £1) with the swaps bank. This fixes the rate for the exchange of principal at maturity.
- There will be a regular (six-monthly) exchange of interest, with the company paying 10% per annum fixed sterling and receiving dollar LIBOR. The interest paid will be 10% on £8 million that amounts to £400,000 every six months.

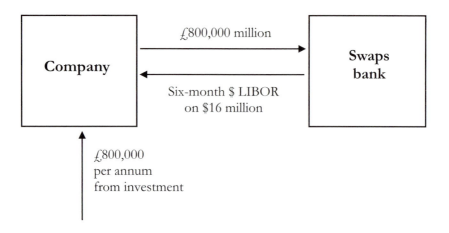

At the end of the swap term (six years), the re-exchange of principal will take place. The investment company exchanges $16 million for £8 million.

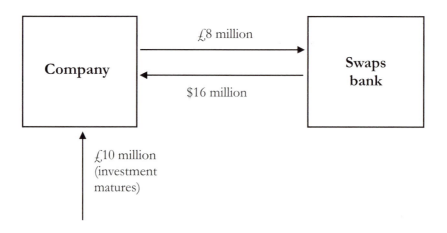

During the life of the swap, US interest rates might increase, as the company originally expected when it made the swap. If dollar LIBOR goes up, the company will receive more in floating rate dollar payments (against its fixed sterling payments) and its dollar income therefore will increase. However, the company's overall return must take account of any change in the sterling/dollar rate over the term of the swap because the company will receive principal in dollars at maturity. If the dollar rises in value, and the exchange rate falls below $2 = £1, the company will benefit because it will receive $16 million in exchange for £8 million sterling at a rate more favorable than the current spot rate.

An alternative arrangement for the swap in this example would be for the investment company to exchange the full amount of the sterling investment for dollars. The principal exchanged would be £10 million and $20 million. (This would allow the company to receive $20 million in six years' time when its £10 million of sterling investments mature.) The company could arrange to pay interest to the swaps bank at 8% or £800,000 per annum, to match its sterling income. However, it would have to make an initial payment to the swaps bank, to compensate for the low rate of interest being paid under the swap agreement.

It is worth noting that to arrange the asset swap on behalf of the investment company, the swaps bank probably would also seek to arrange

- a sterling fixed/floating interest rate swap, and
- a sterling/dollar basis swap.

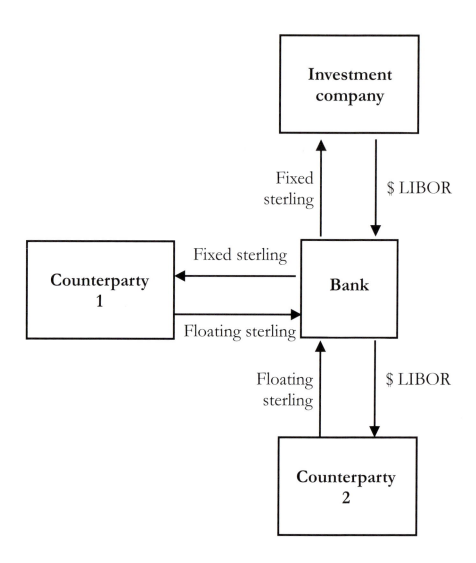

6

Swaps Pricing and the Value of a Swap

Swaps banks try to maintain a continuous two-way liquid market. This allows clients to enter into swaps at a time of their choosing and to reverse existing swaps, if necessary. In a continuous and liquid swaps market, banks must be able to quote prices for a range of maturities. For a company using swaps, it is important to understand how swaps prices might be quoted by a bank.

Swap Rates: Pay Rates and Receive Rates

When a company is negotiating a swap with a bank, the bank will give an indicative fixed rate for the swap, reflecting current market rates of interest. The actual fixed rate will not be determined until the swap agreement is made. A bank's indicative fixed rates will vary according to the period of the swap, as well as with market conditions.

Quoting Prices
It is usual to quote prices for fixed-versus-floating currency swaps using six-month dollar LIBOR as the standard index for the floating rate. This means that for this type of swap, dealers can quote prices simply in terms of the fixed interest rates on the other side of the swap.

Example 1
Delta Bank is prepared to quote the following rates for three-year cross currency interest rate swaps against the dollar.

| Canadian dollars | 6.50-6.75% |
| Sterling | 7.74-7.94% |

Analysis

The quoted rates are the fixed rates that Delta Bank will pay (lower rate) or receive (higher rate) in a cross-currency interest rate swap where the counterparty will receive or pay interest at six-month dollar LIBOR.

The difference between the lower and the higher rate (25 basis points in this example, for the Canadian dollar and 20 basis points for sterling) gives the swap bank a dealing spread on every matching pair of swaps it transacts.

Suppose that Delta Bank transacts a three-year swap in which it receives six-month dollar LIBOR and pays Canadian dollar interest at a fixed rate. The notional principal exchanged is, for example, $100 million and C$140 million. In this transaction, Delta Bank will receive interest at six-month dollar LIBOR and pay interest at a fixed rate of 6.50% on C$140 million.

Suppose that Delta Bank also can transact a matching swap, in which it pays six-month dollar LIBOR on $100 million and receives fixed interest on C$140 million. It will receive a fixed rate of 6.75% on the Canadian dollars.

The spread of 25 basis points (6.75-6.50%) will give the bank a dealing margin of C$350,000 per annum (C$140 million x 0.25%) on its matching pair of swaps.

Example 2

A bank could apply the following prices for fixed rate sterling against six-month dollar LIBOR.

Term (years)	Pay rate	Receive rate
3	8.15%	8.40%
5	8.50%	8.85%
7	8.75%	9.15%
10	9.00%	9.50%

These rates for sterling assume six-monthly payments.

Analysis

The lower rate is the rate that the banks will pay against six-month dollar LIBOR. The higher rate is the fixed rate that the bank would want to receive against payments at six-month dollar LIBOR. If Company A wanted to arrange a five-year swap in which it is a payer of fixed sterling against dollar LIBOR, the bank would want a price of 8.85%. This is the rate it would wish to receive on the sterling principal exchanged, in return for paying Company A dollar LIBOR on the dollar principal. Similarly, if Company B wished to arrange a seven-year swap in which it is a receiver of fixed sterling against dollar LIBOR, the bank would want a price of 8.75% per annum, the bank's pay rate.

Spreads

Fixed pay and receive rates consist of two elements: the bid and offer rates on bonds in the currency, and a swap spread for receiving or paying fixed interest.

- The pay spread is added to the lower offer rate on the bond to obtain a swap pay rate the bank would offer.
- The receive spread is added to the (higher) bid rate on the bond to obtain a swap receive rate the bank would require.

The following table gives swap pay and receive rates for fixed sterling for a range of swap terms. The bank would quote pay and receive spreads, and the appropriate spread would be added to the bond yield when the swap is negotiated to derive the fixed pay or receive rate for the term of the swap. (The bank will quote spreads rather than the full swap rate because the full rate is not determined until the agreement is made, the agreed spread being added to the current bond yield.)

Term	Sterling bond yield		Swap spread		Swap rate	
(years)	Bid	Offer	Pay	Receive	Pay	Receive
	(A)	(B)	(C)	(D)	(B) + (C)	(A)+(D)
2	9.00	8.95	0.60	0.68	9.55	9.68
3	9.10	9.05	0.61	0.69	9.66	9.79
4	9.20	9.15	0.63	0.74	9.78	9.94
5	9.30	9.25	0.65	0.76	9.90	10.06
7	9.40	9.36	0.72	0.87	10.08	10.27
10	9.50	9.46	0.75	0.90	10.21	10.40

If a client negotiates a five-year swap in which he is a receiver of fixed sterling against dollar LIBOR, the bank (as a payer of fixed sterling) would pay 9.90% per annum in return for receiving dollar LIBOR.

Similarly, if a client negotiates a seven-year swap in which the bank is a receiver of fixed sterling against dollar LIBOR, the bank would require interest on the sterling at 10.27% in exchange for paying the dollar LIBOR.

Spread Size
The size of the swap spread above the government bond yield is determined by the supply and demand for swaps. Swap spreads will increase or fall according to how strong (or weak) demand is for swaps in the currency. Influences on supply or demand include the following

- Spreads on swaps will be comparable with the difference between government bond yields and current market yields on debt capital issued by the bank. If the two were inconsistent, it would be cheaper for banks to organize their funding on either the new issues market or the swaps market. Market pressures therefore are towards a convergence of spreads in these two markets.
- Swaps demand could be created by new issues in the eurobond market where the issuer wants to swap the funds it is raising into a different currency (usually the issuer's domestic

currency). In these situations, the bond issuer will want to become a receiver of fixed rate interest in the currency of the bond issue. The effect on swaps prices therefore will be to reduce the swap spread in that currency (i.e. reducing the fixed rate of interest the client will receive).

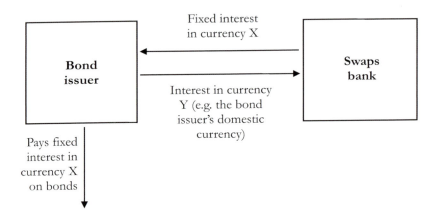

- Expectations of future interest rate levels will influence the extent to which companies want to lock in a fixed rate of interest receivable or payable for the term of the swap. For example, a company will be reluctant to negotiate a swap in which it is a payer of fixed interest on the euro when it expects euro interest rates to fall in the foreseeable future. If other companies share the same expectation the demand for these swaps will drop and the spread will tend to fall in response.

In a liquid swaps market, the spread between the pay and receive rates can be fairly narrow. For currencies where there is very little demand for swaps, spreads will be much wider.

Interest Exchanges

Fixed rates can be quoted for interest paid six monthly, or for interest paid annually. It is standard practice to quote fixed rates for sterling and yen as if interest is paid every six months. For euros and Swiss francs the practice is to quote as if interest is paid annually at the end of each year.

For example, if a bank indicates that the fixed rate for sterling is 10% for a five-year swap, this means a rate of 5% every six months that gives an annualized rate of 10.25%

$$[(1.05)^2 - 1 = 0.01025].$$

Bond Basis and Money Market Basis

Fixed rates can be quoted on either a bond basis (360 days) or a money market basis (365 or 366 days). If a company uses a currency swap with a bond issue, raising funds in one currency and swapping them into a different currency, the fixed interest rate on the swap should be calculated on a bond basis to match the rate on the bond issue.

Bond basis interest = Money market interest x 365/360.

Bond basis interest is a higher figure than interest on a money market basis, to allow for the smaller number of days in the year.

Example
Interest on a money market basis is 10% per annum.

Bond basis interest is therefore

$$10\% \text{ x } 365/360 = 10.14\% \text{ per annum}$$

Value of Currency Swaps
The value of a currency swap is the difference between

- the value of payments receivable (interest and principal), and
- the value of amounts payable.

The value in one currency should be translated into the other currency, to obtain a net valuation.

Value is measured as the present value of the future amounts receivable (or payable), discounted at the current market interest rate for the currency.

Par Swaps

When a swap with no special risk features (a generic swap) is first transacted, its value should be zero. A swap transacted with zero value is called a par swap. Each counterparty receives and pays equal value.

Example

The company Zeta transacts a currency swap with Omega Bank. Zeta is a payer of fixed dollar interest at 5% per annum and a receiver of fixed euro interest at 6% per annum. There is no initial exchange of principal, but principal will be exchanged at maturity, in three years. The principal amounts to be exchanged are $10 million and €8.5 million. The spot dollar/euro rate is €1 = $1.1765. Interest payments in the swap will be exchanged annually.

Analysis

The swap is a par value swap. The cash flows payable and receivable are as follows

Dollars (Principal $10 million)

Year	Item	Amount	Discount rate at 5% per annum	Present value
		$000		$000
1	Interest	500	$\frac{1}{1.05}$	476.19
2	Interest	500	$\frac{1}{1.05^2}$	453.51
3	Interest	500	$\frac{1}{1.05^3}$	431.92
3	Principal	10,000	$\frac{1}{1.05^3}$	8,638.38
Value of dollar cash flows				10,000.00

Euro (Principal €8.5 million)

Year	Item	Amount	Discount rate at 6% per annum	Present value
		€		€ 000
1	Interest	510	$\dfrac{1}{1.06}$	481.13
2	Interest	510	$\dfrac{1}{1.06^2}$	453.90
3	Interest	510	$\dfrac{1}{1.06^3}$	428.21
3	Principal	8,500	$\dfrac{1}{1.06^3}$	7,136.76
Value of euro cash flows				8,500.00

The value of the euro cash flows is €8.5 million. Converted into dollars at the spot rate of $1.1765, this is $10 million, the same as the value of the dollar cash flows. The swap has zero value when transacted.

Non-Par Swaps

Over time, however, a currency swap can develop a value. Changes in interest rates, or in the spot exchange rate, can benefit one counterparty to the disadvantage of the other. The change in value of a swap can be of significance if

- one counterparty wishes to terminate the swap before maturity, by paying the other counterparty the value of the swap, or
- one counterparty wishes to assign his rights and obligations under the terms of the swap to a third party. The value of the swap is exchanged, as a cash payment, between the assignee and assignor.

Termination and assignment are described further in Chapter 7.

Example

Suppose that in the example on page 69 soon after the swap has been transacted, the dollar interest rate goes up from 5% to 5.25%, and the euro/dollar exchange rate changes to €1 = $1.15.

Analysis

The present value of the dollar payments now will be as follows

Year	Item	Amount	Discount rate at 5%	Present value
		$000		$000
1	Interest	500	$\dfrac{1}{1.0525}$	475.059
2	Interest	500	$\dfrac{1}{1.0525^2}$	451.363
3	Interest	500	$\dfrac{1}{1.0525^3}$	428.848
3	Principal	10,000	$\dfrac{1}{1.0525^3}$	8,576.966
Revised value of dollar cash flows				9,932.236

The present value of the euro cash flows in the swap is unchanged at €8.5 million, but at the new exchange rate of €1 = $1.15, the euro value of these cash flows is €8,636,727 ($9,932,263 ÷ 1.15).

The currency swap's value is now:

	€
Value of dollar cash flows	8,636,727
Value of euro cash flows	8,500,000
Net value	136,727

The currency swap has a positive value to the counterparty receiving the dollar payments and paying euros, because the value of the dollar cash flows now exceeds the value of the euro cash flows.

Swaps can be transacted with a non-par value at the outset. A non-generic swap could incorporate special features that modify its value, or could be deliberately priced at off-market interest rates to suit the requirements of one of the swap counterparties. In these cases, an upfront cash payment is made by one counterparty to the other, when the swap is transacted, to provide compensation to cover the value of the swap.

7

Why Use Swaps?

Currency swaps can serve several purposes:

- to arrange finance by means of swaps and bond issues
- to hedge a longer-term currency exposure
- to alter the currency of investment income.

Arranging Finance

Currency swaps often are arranged in conjunction with a bond issue. The company or institution issuing the bonds can use a currency swap to issue debt in one currency and then swap the proceeds into the currency it desires. This allows companies to access a larger investor base by issuing in overseas markets in a currency that has more appeal to those investors, and then swapping.

For example, a company can raise funds in dollars and swap them into Swiss francs, either by exchanging principal at the near-value date (swapping borrowed dollars for francs) or by selling the borrowed dollars in the spot FX markets in exchange for the Swiss francs.

Swap to Arrange Finance

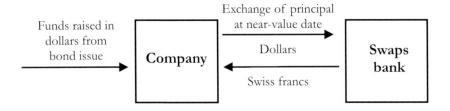

Interest payments under this swap arrangement will be as follows

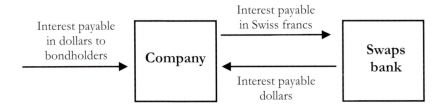

The company, having obtained finance in Swiss francs under the swap, should earn sufficient income in Swiss francs to meet the payments to the swaps bank. Dollar receipts under the swap arrangement would offset the company's interest payments to its bondholders.

At the end of the swap term, there will be a re-exchange of principal.

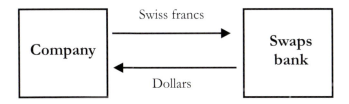

The company's payment in Swiss francs to the swaps bank should be financed out of its income from investments in that currency over the term of the swap. The receipt of principal in dollars could be used to redeem the company's bonds.

There are three specific purposes for arranging a swap with a bond issue.

● *To obtain lower cost funds.* When market conditions are suitable, it is possible to raise funds in one currency and swap the funds into the desired currency to produce a lower net interest cost than by directly borrowing the desired currency. This is a feature of many eurobond issues. If, for example, there is strong (short-term) demand for investments in currency A, a company seeking to borrow in currency B could exploit a window of opportunity and issue bonds in currency A at a low rate of interest and swap them into the desired currency B. This is possible only if market interest rates permit such an opportunity to be exploited. Swaps banks will advise corporate clients on the availability of cheaper funding opportunities. Because these opportunities are temporary, when they occur companies might have to opt for a bond issue at a time that isn't necessarily their most preferred.

● *To gain access to a restricted capital market.* If a company cannot raise funds in a particular capital market, it could arrange a swap with a bank that does have access to the market. Bond markets for some currencies are more difficult to access than others. For example, companies and other organizations wishing to issue yen bonds must have a high credit rating. A company without the minimum required credit rating might issue bonds in one currency (typically dollars) and arrange a swap and convert its liability into yen.

● *To obtain funding in a form not otherwise available.* Market conditions might preclude the issuance of long-term debt bearing a fixed interest charge in, for example, Japanese yen. It may be possible to issue long-term fixed rate debt in dollars, and swap it into yen to create a surrogate long-term fixed rate yen loan.

Example

Two multinational companies, Gamma and Delta, are both seeking to raise funds with a five-year new debt issue. Gamma has a higher credit rating than Delta. Interest rates that each company could obtain for five-year borrowings are as follows

	Government 5-year bond yield	Gamma Cost of debt issue	Delta Cost of debt issue
Sterling	10%	10.40%	10.80%
Dollar	7%	7.30%	7.40%

It would cost Delta 0.40% per annum more than Gamma to raise funds in sterling (10.80 - 10.40), but only 0.10% per annum more than Gamma to raise funds in dollars. The difference in Delta's excess borrowing costs between dollars and sterling is 0.30% (0.40 - 0.10). This can be shared out in a swap arrangement that gives Gamma and Delta a lower borrowing cost, and the swap bank a net revenue on two legs of a swap arrangement. Gamma wants to borrow in dollars and Delta wants to borrow in sterling. Both want fixed rate financing.

Analysis
Delta would have to pay 0.40% per annum more than Gamma to borrow in sterling, whereas in dollars, it would have to pay only 0.10% more. Gamma therefore has a comparative advantage over Delta in borrowing in sterling, but it wants to borrow in dollars. A currency swap creates an opportunity for lower-cost funding for both companies.

- Delta can borrow in dollars and Gamma can borrow an equivalent amount in sterling.
- By means of swap transactions, both companies could switch the currency of their liability, Delta into sterling and Gamma into dollars.

A swaps bank, for example, Alpha Bank, would negotiate a swap with each company to achieve this result. If the spot exchange rate is $2 = £1, the exchange of principal in each swap market would be £10 million for $20 million.

Exchange of Principal: Near-Value Date

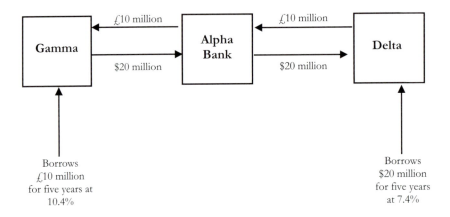

Gamma wants to borrow dollars at a fixed rate, and in its swap arrangement therefore will wish to be a payer of fixed dollars against fixed sterling. Delta wants to borrow in sterling, and its swap position will be as a payer of fixed sterling against fixed dollars.

Alpha Bank might agree to the following rates

- Gamma to receive 10.40% per annum fixed on £10 million and to pay 7.20% per annum fixed on $20 million

- Delta to receive 7.40% per annum fixed on $20 million and to pay 10.70% per annum fixed on £10 million.

As a consequence, Gamma will pay 7.20% per annum on its dollars, 0.10% per annum less than it could obtain directly in the new issues market. Similarly, Delta will pay 10.70% per annum on sterling, also 0.10% per annum less than in the new issues market. Alpha Bank will make a loss of 0.20% per annum on the dollars (7.20 - 7.40) but a profit of 0.30% per annum on the sterling (10.70 - 10.40).

Exchange of Interest

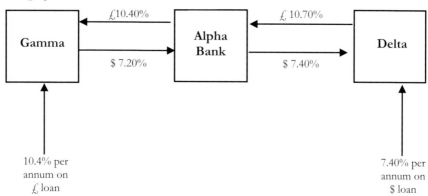

The Full Cost of Swaps with Bond Issues

Swaps can be arranged to suit the individual requirements of the client. If the client is issuing a bond in one currency, and wants to arrange a swap in a different currency, it may want to negotiate a swap whereby its receipts are an *exact* match of its payments on the bond. The following example is fairly complex, and you will need some understanding of discounting and present values to follow it.

Example
Sphere Bank and CC International enter a five-year currency swap agreement in which Sphere Bank pays Swiss francs at a fixed rate of 5.25% per annum bond and CC International pays dollars at a fixed rate of 8.50% per annum bond.

CC International issues a five-year bond of SFr100 million, with interest payable at 5% per annum. Issue fees are 2%. It wishes to swap its Swiss franc liability for a dollar liability, but the swaps bank does not want an initial exchange of principal.

Analysis
CC International will want to receive interest and principal under the swap agreement to meet its obligations to its bondholders as illustrated in the column headed *Cash flow required to cover bond obligations* in the following table.

Receiving Swiss Francs at 5.25% p.a. under a Swap Agreement

Year	Cash flow required to cover bond obligations	Discount rate at 5.25% of cash flows	Present value of cash flows
	SFr		SFr
1	5,000,000	÷ 1.0525	4,750,594
2	5,000,000	÷ $(1.0525)^2$	4,513,628
3	5,000,000	÷ $(1.0525)^3$	4,288,483
4	5,000,000	÷ $(1.0525)^4$	4,074,568
5	105,000,000	÷ $(1.0525)^5$	81,297,794
			98,925,067

CC International can arrange with Sphere Bank for its receipts to match its required cash flow profile. Sphere Bank will calculate a present value of the cash flows by discounting them at its swap pay rate of 5.25% per annum. These calculations are shown above, and the today-value to Sphere Bank of the Swiss franc payments it will make to CC International are SFr98,925,067. This would be the bank's cost for servicing the required cash flows to CC International at an interest of 5.25%.

The bank would apply the spot dollar/Swiss franc rate to determine the amount of notional dollar principal for the swap. If the spot rate is SFr1.50 = $1, the notional dollar principal for the swap will be $65,950,044 (98,925,067 ÷ 1.50).

The bank therefore will expect to receive, under the swap agreement, interest at 8.50% on $65,950,044.

Year		Cash flow required by Sphere Bank
1	(8.50% of $65,950,044)	5,605,754
2		5,605,754
3		5,605,754
4		5,605,754
5	(5,605,754 + 65,950,044)	71,555,798

Because there is no initial exchange of principal at the near-value date,

CC International will raise SFr98 million net of issue costs and sell these for dollars at the spot rate of SFr1.50 = $1 to raise $65,333,333.

The net result of the swap for CC International is that it will raise $65,333,333 in cash, and pay the dollar cash flows under the swap. Its Swiss franc income under the swap will be sufficient to match its payments on the bond.

Summary: CC International's Cash Flows

Year	Cash from bond converted to dollars $	Bond payments SFr	Swap receive SFr	Swap pay $
0	65,333,333			
1		-5,000,000	5,000,000	-5,605,754
2		-5,000,000	5,000,000	-5,605,754
3		-5,000,000	5,000,000	-5,605,754
4		-5,000,000	5,000,000	-5,605,754
5		-	105,000,000	-
		105,000,00	0	71,555,798

The actual cost to the company for the dollars raised in cash can be calculated (by discounted cash flow) to be about 8.75% per annum.

The actual amount received under the swap is SFr5,193,566. However, SFr5,000,000 is paid that represents the amount needed to meet the bond cash flows. The additional amount is placed on deposit. At an assumed rate of 5.25% over five years, this will be sufficient to meet the difference between the maturing bond obligation of SFr100,000,000 and the Swiss francs received from the swap of SFr98,925,067.

Access to Currency Funding
Currency swaps sometimes can give a borrower access to funding in a currency that it cannot borrow directly. Direct borrowing in a currency can be difficult for a company when

- the bond markets in the currency are illiquid, and successful bond issues are difficult to arrange
- the company does not have a recognized name or a sufficient credit rating to borrow in the currency's domestic bond market or in the eurobond market.

Example

A Dutch company, AVB NV, is planning a programme of investments in the US and wants to borrow dollars to do this. Given the current state of the bond markets, it could borrow in euro for five-years at 7%, but could not borrow in dollars, either in the US bond markets or in the eurobond market. Five-year dollar/euro swaps are being quoted at 5.00-5.225% for fixed interest dollars and at 7.20-7.40% for euro.

Analysis

AVB could borrow in euro for five years at 7%, and convert these into dollars for investing. It also can transact a dollar/euro currency swap, paying fixed dollars and receiving fixed euro. The notional principal in euro could be the same as the amount of euros borrowed.

AVB will pay interest at 5.225% on the notional amount of dollars, and receive 7.20% on the corresponding amount of euro. Because the interest payable on the euro will be just 7%, there will be a gain of 20 basis points (7.20-7%).

Summary

Loan	-7.00 in euros
Swap	
Receive	+7.20 in euros
Arbitrage gain	+0.20 in euros
Swap	
Pay	-5.225 in dollars
Net cost	5.225% in dollars
Less	0.20% in euros

Credit Arbitrage

Arbitrage is the process of exploiting price differences between two products or two markets to make an immediate and certain profit. Credit arbitrage opportunities arise when two companies each can borrow in two or more markets, but at interest rates that are comparatively better for one borrower on one market and for the other borrower in the second market.

Credit arbitrage opportunities

	Market 1 (e.g. $) Borrowing costs	Market 2 (e.g. yen) Borrowing costs
Company Alpha	v%	y%
Company Beta	x%	z%
Borrowing cost differential	(v - x)%	(y - z)%

Credit arbitrage could be possible if $(v - x) > (y - z)$, or $(v - x) < (y - z)$.

In the table above, Alpha can borrow dollars at v% and yen at y%. Beta can borrow dollars at x% and yen at z%. If the difference in their dollar borrowing costs $(v - x)$ is greater or smaller than the difference in their yen borrowing costs $(y - z)$, credit arbitrage by means of a currency swap could be possible, to reduce the cost of borrowing.

Suppose that the borrowing costs of Alpha and Beta are as follows

	$	Yen
	%	%
Alpha	5.0	4.2
Beta	6.4	4.8
Difference	1.4	0.6

Suppose also that Alpha wants to borrow yen and Beta wants to borrow dollars.

Alpha could borrow the currency where its cost of borrowing is comparatively cheaper. This is dollars that it can borrow at 1.4% less than Beta. Beta could borrow the currency where its cost of borrowing is relatively less expensive. This is yen that it can borrow at just 0.6% more than Alpha.

The two companies then can arrange a currency swap, in which they share the benefits of the 0.8% lower net costs (1.4% - 0.6%). If a bank acts as intermediary in the swap arrangements, its profit also could come from a share of this 0.8% pool of benefits.

The following examples illustrate how swaps can be used for credit arbitrage, to the benefit of both borrowers.

Example 1
Stateside Inc, a US corporation, wants to borrow seven-year funds in sterling. Blight plc, a UK company, wants to borrow seven-year funds in dollars. They can raise seven-year funds on the domestic bond or eurobond markets at the following rates

	Dollar funds	Sterling funds
	%	%
Stateside Inc	5.1	7.8
Blight plc	6.0	8.0

Both companies have approached Omega Bank. Stateside has indicated a desire to raise about £20 million at a cost of funds not exceeding 7.5% per annum. Similarly, Blight wishes to borrow about $30 million, but at a cost of 5.85% or less. The sterling/dollar spot rate is $1.50 = £1.

Analysis
Stateside can borrow dollars at a rate 0.9% below the cost of dollar borrowing for Blight, and can borrow sterling at just 0.2% below the cost of sterling borrowing for Blight.

This difference (in borrowing differentials) creates a possibility of cheaper borrowing through a swap arrangement. The ability to transact a swap, however, depends on the rates that a swap bank will agree to.

Stateside

Stateside can raise $30 million in the bond markets at 5.1%. It can then arrange a sterling/dollar swap for $30 million/£20 million. Stateside will wish to receive at least 5.1% fixed in dollars, and pay no more than 7.5% fixed in sterling.

Blight

Blight can raise £20 million in the bond markets at 8.0%, and arrange a sterling/dollar swap for $30 million/£20 million. Blight will wish to receive at least 8.0% in sterling and pay no more than 5.85% in dollars.

Omega Bank

The bank could accommodate the requirements of both companies as follows

These swaps would satisfy the minimum requirements of each company, leaving Stateside with net payments of 7.5% fixed in sterling and Blight with net payments of 5.85% fixed in dollars. The net position of Omega Bank from the matching swaps would be as follows

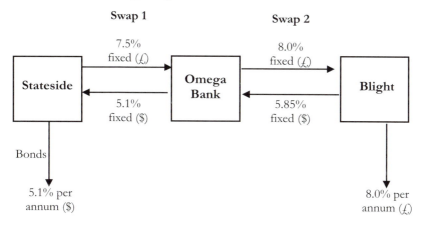

Omega Bank

		Dollars		Sterling
Swap 1	Pay	-5.10%	Receive	+7.50%
Swap 2	Receive	+5.85%	Pay	-8.00%
Net	Receive	+0.75%	Pay	-0.50%

Omega Bank will make a net surplus in dollars but a net deficit in sterling. It will have to decide whether a suitable dealing margin can be made from the swaps, and negotiate with the two companies on this basis.

Example 2

Stars and Stripes Inc (S&S), a US corporation, wants to raise five-year funds in Swiss francs at a fixed rate. Saxen, a Swiss company, wants to borrow five-year dollar funds at a floating rate.

They can borrow at the following rates:

	Dollars	**Swiss francs**
S&S Inc	US LIBOR + 0.125%	6.25%
Saxen	US LIBOR + 0.75%	6.20%

S&S wants the maximum cost of its Swiss franc funding to be 6%, and Saxen wants to borrow at no more than USLIBOR + 0.50%.

Analysis

S&S can borrow dollars more cheaply than Saxen, by 0.625% per annum (0.75% - 0.125%). Saxen can borrow Swiss francs more cheaply than S&S (by 0.05% per annum). This creates scope for interest rate arbitrage through currency swaps.

A swap bank might be able to match the two swaps (e.g. by transacting swaps with each company for the same principal amounts). S&S would borrow in dollars at a floating rate and Saxen would borrow fixed Swiss francs.

The matched swaps then could be arranged as follows

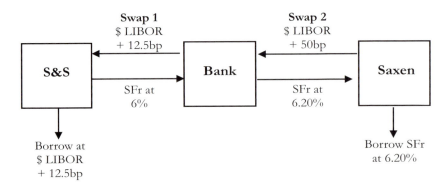

Both companies would achieve their funding at the required cost.

The net position for Omega Bank would be as follows

Omega Bank

		Dollars	Swiss francs	
Swap 1	Pay	- (LIBOR + 0.125)%	Receive	6.0%
Swap 2	Receive	+ (LIBOR + 0.500)%	Pay	6.2%
Net	Receive	0.375%	Pay	0.2%

The bank should decide whether these matching transactions that would yield a surplus of 0.375% per annum in dollars but a deficit of 0.20% per annum in Swiss francs, would provide it with a satisfactory dealing margin.

Credit Arbitrage and Market Liquidity
The scope for credit arbitrage usually is greater for currencies in which there is a large swaps market.

Example
Some years ago, a Canadian bank's Australian subsidiary made an issue of C$100 million eurobonds and swapped into dollars (paying a floating rate linked to dollar LIBOR).

The swap enabled the bank to raise dollar funds more cheaply than by borrowing dollars direct. However, the bank would have preferred to swap the Canadian dollars into Australian dollars. It was unable to do this because there was insufficient demand in the Australian dollar swap market, except at high rates of interest. The small size of the Australian dollar market, and the consequent high prices, made credit arbitrage unachievable.

Hedging Currency Exposures

Currency swaps can be used as an instrument for hedging longer-term exposures to currency risk. Currency risk that is described in detail in the introductory book in this series called *Currency Risk Management*, is the risk of losses from adverse exchange rate movements. Long-term exposures to currency risk arise in a number of situations.

- If a company has a long-term investment in a currency that generates a stream of regular income, there will be an exposure to a fall in the value of the currency. This will reduce the value, in the investor's domestic currency, of both the income from the investment and the investment's capital value.
- If a company has a long-term liability in a foreign currency, such as a term loan, but no regular income in that currency, it will be at risk from an increase in the currency's value that would make the loan more costly to service.
- If a company expects to make a foreign currency payment or to receive foreign currency income at some time in the longer term, it will be at risk from a change in the value of the currency in the exposure period up to the time of the payment or receipt. A rise in the value of the currency would increase the cost of any such payment, and a fall in the currency would reduce the value of any such receipt.

A currency exposure can be hedged (reduced or eliminated) either by creating a matching and opposite stream of cash flows, or by locking in an exchange rate now for a future receipt or payment of currency.

If a company has a foreign currency investment, a hedge can be created by setting up a stream of payments in the currency to match the stream of investment income. Similarly, if a company has a foreign currency debt, a hedge can be provided by setting up a stream of regular income in the currency to match the interest payments on the loan.

Matching cash inflows and outflows in a currency provides a hedge because any change in the value of the currency will result in equal and offsetting gains and losses. If the value of income in the currency falls, so too will the cost of payments; if the cost of payments goes up, so too will the value of the matched income.

Example

A multinational owns a subsidiary that extracts minerals in Australia for sale both domestically and in the US. All expenditures are in Australian dollars, but sales to the US are priced in dollars. The company, that is partly funded by fixed rate loans in Australian dollars, is concerned about the currency exposures arising from its dollar income, and is seeking a way of hedging them.

Pre-Swap Cash Flows

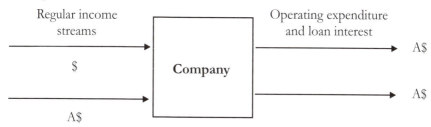

It does not want to borrow extra funds for its operations, this means that obtaining a loan in dollars (so that interest payments on the dollar loan can be used to offset the dollar trading income) will not be a suitable hedge in this case.

Analysis

One method of hedging the dollar exposure would be to arrange a currency swap. The company has a loan in Australian dollars. By swapping some or all of this Australian dollar liability for a dollar liability, with regular dollar interest payments, it can hedge its dollar income without borrowing dollar funds. In the swap agreement the company would receive fixed Australian dollars against dollars.

Under the swap arrangement, the company will pay interest in dollars, probably at a variable rate linked to LIBOR. These payments will create a hedge for the company's dollar income. The company will receive interest under the swap arrangement in Australian dollars, probably at a fixed rate, that will help to cover Australian dollar expenditure for interest on the loan and operating expenses.

This example has not yet considered the amount of principal in the swap agreement. As part of its hedging strategy, the company should try to ensure that the interest payments in dollars to the swaps bank, plus the final payment of principal in dollars at the end of the swap agreement, are matched sufficiently by the dollar income from export sales. Deciding on an appropriate principal amount calls for judgment, and the company should continue to monitor its dollar exposures after a swap agreement has been made in order to assess whether further hedging action should be taken.

Swap to Hedge Currency Exposures

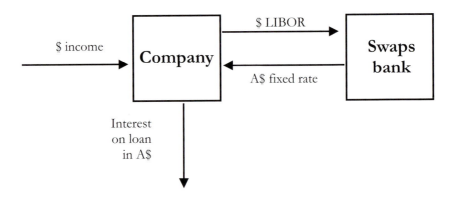

Exercise 1

See if you can formulate a solution to the following problem

Foxtrot plc, a UK company, has made a five-year dollar bond issue for $60 million, paying interest at a fixed rate of 6% per annum (with six-monthly interest payments). All its revenue from operations is in sterling, and the company wants to arrange a five-year currency swap to hedge its exposure to the dollar.

The spot sterling/dollar rate is $1.50 = £1.

Required

Recommend the type of currency swap that is most appropriate if

- Foxtrot expects sterling interest rates to rise or remain fairly stable over the next five years
- Foxtrot expects sterling interest rates to fall over the next five years.

Solution

Foxtrot can hedge its risk by transacting a five-year currency swap. The company will receive dollars and pay sterling.

Receiving dollars

Foxtrot should receive fixed interest payments in dollars. Ideally, the receipts of dollars should match the company's dollar payments on the bonds, i.e. $1.8 million interest every six months (3% of $60 million) and $60 million at maturity. This would enable the company to create a perfect hedge against its exposure to dollar payments on the bonds. The dollar receipts profile should be negotiated with the swap bank.

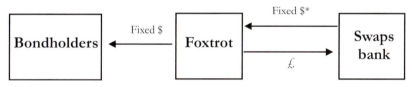

* Ideally, matched amounts

Paying sterling

Foxtrot will wish to pay sterling.

- If it expects interest rates to go up (or remain stable) it should arrange to pay fixed interest.
- If it expects interest rates to fall, it should arrange to pay in sterling at a floating rate (six-month sterling LIBOR). If Foxtrot is correct, and sterling interest rates fall over the next five years, it will make lower interest payments in the swap as the LIBOR rate comes down.

If Foxtrot can match fixed dollar income from the swap with fixed dollar payments on the bonds, it will create a hedge against any movement in the sterling/dollar rate and therefore will eliminate its currency risk.

Exercise 2

Now try to find your own solution to this problem and check it with the one that follows.

Zetacorp is a large multinational that wishes to raise about $20 million of floating rate debt for a five-year term. It can raise this money at six month dollar LIBOR + 50 basis points (0.50%). The swaps team of Azure Bank has discussed these funding requirements with the company and has suggested making a Swiss franc eurobond issue at a low interest rate, combined with a swap into floating rate dollars. The exchange of principal will be at the current spot rate of SFr1.51 = $1. Azure Bank's fixed Swiss franc swap rates are 4.90-5.03 (pay rate and receive rate) for a five-year swap. The company could issue five year Swiss franc bonds at 4.85%.

How would a swap be arranged and what, if any, would be the annual savings for Zetacorp?

Solution

Zetacorp could make a Swiss franc bond issue for SFr26.67 million at 4.85% and exchange this into dollars at SFr1.51 = $1 at the near-value date.

The exchange of interest in the swap would involve Zetacorp receiving Swiss franc interest at the bank's pay rate of 4.90%, and the payment of dollar LIBOR. After five years, at the end of the swap agreement, there will be a re-exchange of principal, and Zetacorp would use the Swiss francs to redeem the bonds at maturity.

This is illustrated on the next page.

Zetacorp will profit in two ways

● It will make a Swiss franc profit on the difference between the rate paid on the bonds (4.85%) and the rate received under the swap (4.90%). This profit will total 0.05% of SFr26.67 million each year, i.e. SFr13,332.80.

● It will save 0.50% per annum on the cost of its dollar borrowing, because it will pay dollar LIBOR under the swap compared with dollar LIBOR +0.50% if it borrowed dollars directly. This will create an annual saving of $100,000 (0.50% of $20 million).

Zetacorp Currency Swap

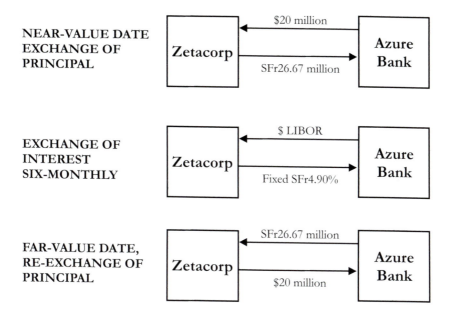

NEAR-VALUE DATE EXCHANGE OF PRINCIPAL — Zetacorp ← $20 million — Azure Bank; Zetacorp → SFr26.67 million → Azure Bank

EXCHANGE OF INTEREST SIX-MONTHLY — Zetacorp ← $ LIBOR — Azure Bank; Zetacorp → Fixed SFr4.90% → Azure Bank

FAR-VALUE DATE, RE-EXCHANGE OF PRINCIPAL — Zetacorp ← SFr26.67 million — Azure Bank; Zetacorp → $20 million → Azure Bank

Locking in a Forward Rate

Currency swaps can be used to lock in a forward rate for a future foreign currency receipt or payment, either as an alternative to a forward exchange contract, or when a forward contract is unobtainable.

For the following example, assume a swap period of just one year. (A short period helps to illustrate the significance of the interest payments within a swap arrangement.)

Example 1
Company A expects to make a payment of $5 million in one year's time. The spot sterling/dollar rate is $1.48 and the 12-month forward premium is 2.10 cents. The one-year interest rate is 5.5% for sterling and 4% for the dollar. The one-year forward rate is $1.4590 ($1.48 - 0.021), with the dollar worth more forward than spot against sterling.

Analysis
Alternative 1: Forward contract. A forward contract to purchase $5 million would cost £3,427,005 (5 million ÷ 1.4590).

Alternative 2: A swap arrangement (with no exchange of principal at the near-value date). company A wants to receive $5 million in one year to make the payment. Under a swap arrangement

- at the end of one year, company A would receive $5 million from a counterparty bank, and would pay £3,378,378 (at the current spot rate of $1.48).
- interest would be exchanged, with company A paying sterling at 5.5% on £3,378,378 to the bank (£185,811) and the bank paying dollars at 4% on $5 million to company A ($200,000).

Net effect

	£
Interest exchange	
Company A pays	-185,811
Company A receives$200,000 (at $1.4590 to £1, for example)	+137,080
	-48,731
Net cost	
Principal exchange at maturity	-3,378,378
Total cost of $5 million	-3,427,109

Although the exchange rate into sterling of company A's dollar interest receipts cannot be predicted accurately, the swap effectively locks in a cost for the $5 million similar to the cost of a forward contract.

Example 2

A UK company forecasts that it will have a large income stream of $60 million in five years' time. Its treasurer is considering the use of a swap to hedge the exposure.

A bank indicates that it would be willing to arrange a swap.

- The company will receive $60 million from its trading transactions in five years' time, and wants to fix a rate for converting this into sterling. This can be done by arranging for the exchange of principal under the swap at the far-value date, with the company exchanging its dollar income into sterling. The agreed rate is the current spot rate of $1.50 = £1.

- The six-monthly interest flows under the swap agreement go the same way as the exchange of principal at the far-value date. The company will pay interest in dollars (at a variable rate, six-month LIBOR) and will receive interest at a fixed rate in sterling. Let's suppose that this fixed rate is 6% per annum (3% six-monthly).

Currency Swap to Lock in a Forward in a Forward Rate

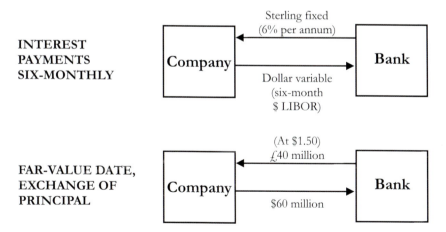

The company could hedge its six-monthly interest payments in dollars over the term of the swap, either structurally by offsetting the expenditures against other dollar income from its overseas or export operations, or by a series of forward market purchases timed to mature at six-monthly intervals. Alternatively, it could opt for a single settlement of the rolled-up interest differential at the end of the swap arrangement, with no interest payments until the maturity date.

Exercise

Try to find your own solution to this problem. Illustrate the swap exchanges with a box-and-arrows diagram, showing the amount of principal exchanged and the swap rates of interest.

A large company expects to have to make a trade payment of $23 million in three years. Its treasurer wishes to hedge the exposure and is discussing a swap transaction with a bank. The bank would agree to an exchange of principal at the current spot rate. (Assume this is $1.4375 = £1.) For a three-year swap agreement the bank would pay 7% and wants to receive 7.4% against six-month dollar LIBOR.

Solution

The company needs to pay dollars for a transaction in three years' time, and will want to receive dollars in the exchange of principal, under the swap agreement, at the far-value date.

The company therefore would be a payer of fixed sterling against LIBOR. The bank wants to receive 7.4% per annum fixed for sterling.

The swap agreement provides for an initial exchange of principal, with the company buying $23 million spot and exchanging it into sterling at the same rate ($1.4375 to £1).

Reversals, Terminations and Assignments

Currency swaps would not be widely used if they weren't flexible and resulted in a client being tied to a long-term financial management strategy that, once made, would be difficult to alter. The liquidity of the swap market means that a company can cancel a swap position if it wants. The swaps bank will be able to adjust its own position and avoid exposure to extra risk from a client changing its position.

Most swaps, once transacted, continue until the re-exchange of principal at the end of their term. When a client's circumstances change, however, so that the swap no longer suits its requirements, it can unwind its position by

- reversing the original position
- terminating the swap
- assigning the swap.

Reversing the Original Position

A swap counterparty can transact a second swap with flows in the opposite direction. For example, suppose that a company enters into a six-year swap agreement in which it is a payer of fixed sterling against dollar LIBOR. If two years later it wanted to eliminate its swap position, it could transact another swap agreement (with either the same bank or a different bank) with a four-year term in which it is a receiver of fixed sterling against dollar LIBOR. Because the spot rate of exchange and interest rates will be different when the second swap is transacted, the company will face gains or losses. For example, if in the first swap the company is a payer of fixed sterling at 6.5% and in the second swap is a receiver of fixed sterling at 6% on the same principal amount, there would be a net loss on interest of 0.5% per annum for each of the next four years until both swaps mature.

Solution to Exercise

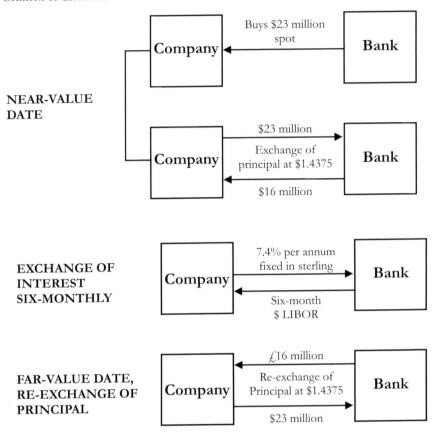

NEAR-VALUE DATE

Company — Buys $23 million spot ← Bank

Company — $23 million → / Exchange of principal at $1.4375 / ← $16 million — Bank

EXCHANGE OF INTEREST SIX-MONTHLY

Company — 7.4% per annum fixed in sterling → / ← Six-month $ LIBOR — Bank

FAR-VALUE DATE, RE-EXCHANGE OF PRINCIPAL

Company — ← £16 million / Re-exchange of Principal at $1.4375 / $23 million → — Bank

Terminating the Swap

A party to a swap wishing to eliminate its swap position can ask the swap bank (the counterparty) to terminate the agreement, that the bank would do. If market interest rates were to have moved so that the swap rates were not advantageous to the bank, it would make a payment to the counterparty for the termination (less a termination fee). If market interest rates were to have moved the other way, the termination costs would include a compensation payment to the bank. The termination payment (excluding the compensation element) would be based on the value of the swap at the termination date. The value of currency swaps is explained in Chapter 6.

Assignment

Occasionally, a currency swap is assigned to a new counterparty by one of the original counterparties. Assignment is an alternative option to early termination when one of the counterparties wishes to cancel his or her future obligations under a swap contract. In an assignment, the new counterparty (the assignee) takes over from the original counterparty in the swap (the assignor). Swap assignments also are called a swap sale or swap buyout.

For reasons of credit risk, the other counterparty to the swap must approve the assignee.

A cash payment is made on assignment, equal to the currency value of the swap. The payment could be from assignee to assignor or vice versa, depending on whether the swap has a positive or negative value.

Advantages of Currency Swaps

For companies large enough to use them, currency swaps have several potential advantages.

- They can be arranged in currencies where long-dated forward contracts are not easily arranged. This is because of the bank's concern that its customer might fail to honor a forward contract at maturity, leaving the bank exposed to currency risk from the dishonored transaction. With currency swaps, in contrast, the regular exchange of interest payments over the term of the swap (combined with the agreement to re-exchange principal at the same rate as the initial exchange of principal at the near-value date) reduces the risk to the bank. Banks therefore are more comfortable transacting swaps than they are for long-dated forward contracts, even though there is some interest rate and currency risk with swaps. (Interest rate risk occurs when market interest rates change during the period of the swap so that the rates the swaps bank pays or receives becomes less favorable than current market rates.)

- They can be used to hedge longer-dated transaction exposures and economic exposures, and might provide more favorable terms than a longer-dated forward contract. Swap spreads, being interest-rate driven, tend to be tighter than spreads for higher-risk FX forward contracts.

8

Arranging a Swap

Although the currency swaps market is still confined to relatively few participants, documentation in now widely standardized, and there are regulations and unofficial codes of conduct.

Who Uses Currency Swaps?

A large proportion of currency swaps are transacted between banks. Other organizations arranging swaps with a bank include sovereign institutions, public sector corporations, supranational organizations such as the World Bank and the European Investment Bank, and very large companies with quasi-banking capabilities. The minimum economic dealing size is several million pounds value and, coupled with the sophistication of the market, make swaps unsuitable for small companies.

Banks are active in the swaps market in two ways

- as an intermediary between two counterparties
- as an end-counterparty, in order to manage their own funding or investment requirements.

Swap Banks
Banks that operate as intermediaries in the currency swap market could act as

- arrangers
- matched book dealers
- market makers.

In an arrangement, a bank identifies and introduces two matching counterparties who then transact the swap directly. The arranging bank charges a fee to each counterparty for its service.

A matched book dealer identifies two customers with matching swap requirements and acts as counterparty to each customer in two separate (but matching) swap agreements. Customers prefer to transact a swap with a bank because the perceived credit risk is much lower. Matched book dealers make a profit on the dealing spread, and also charge each counterparty an arrangement fee.

Arrangement

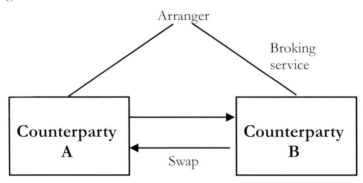

Matched Book Dealing

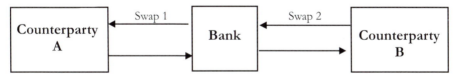

A market maker in swaps will be willing to transact swaps in reasonable amounts with a customer, without a matching swap being immediately available. The market maker will aim to run a broadly matched book in swaps, but will tolerate temporary exposure to risk on unmatched swap positions. Market makers

- will manage their swaps book as a portfolio, monitoring the aggregate position rather than matching individual swaps, and

- are more easily able to arrange multi-legged swaps.

Usually market makers do not charge an arrangement fee, and make their profit from the dealing spread.

The major swaps banks have formed the International Swaps and Derivatives Association (ISDA) to represent their market and to standardize practices and documentation.

Brokers

Brokers or agents arrange currency swap deals between counterparties, but do not act as a counterparty themselves. The role of a broker or agent is to

- identify favorable opportunities for arranging swaps
- discuss possible swap transactions with potential counterparties
- secure the best mutually beneficial terms for the counterparties.

(A broker is an organization that does not act as principal in any transaction. An agent is an organization that will sometimes act as principal/counterparty in a bond market or swap market transaction.)

Brokers receive a fee that is paid when the swap transaction is made. The fee typically is one basis point (applied to the size of the deal) from each counterparty.

To carry out their function, brokers need to take swap prices from their customers continuously, and make these available to others. This is done by posting swap prices on to information networks such as Reuters, where brokers have their own screens. Screen prices are indicative only. If a customer wishes to transact a swap at a price quoted, he should contact the broker directly to secure a firm price.

Negotiating a Transaction

The currency swap market is an over-the-counter market, with most dealing conducted by telephone. Indicative swap prices are published on screen-based information systems (e.g. Reuters). The main financial details for a currency swap are agreed verbally, and confirmed by an exchange of fax or SWIFT messages, usually within 24 hours. The swap is then documented and signed, and contracts exchanged.

Swap Documentation
The contract document sets out the financial details of the swap, and the rights of both parties to enforce the contract, for example in an event of default.

The key elements in a swap agreement are

- the amount of each currency (and so the rate for the exchange of principal)
- interest payment arrangements, specifying interest rates payable and the dates on which interest is payable
- conditions under which one counterparty to the swap would be considered in default
- conditions under which the swap can be terminated
- damages payable in the event of default, or compensation arrangements in the event of termination.

To simplify and reduce the cost of swaps documentation, initiatives were introduced by

- the International Swaps and Derivatives Association (ISDA) and
- the British Bankers Association (BBA).

ISDA Documentation

ISDA has developed a comprehensive standardization of swaps

documentation, for both interest rate and currency swaps, and most swaps are now based on the standard documentation: 1992 ISDA Master Agreement (Multicurrency - Cross Border).

ISDA master contracts provide the basic terms and conditions of a swap. Once a master agreement has been reached between two counterparties, all subsequent swap transactions between them become subject to the terms and conditions of the master agreement. Each new swap transaction between the counterparties is added to the master agreement as an appendix.

ISDA master agreements primarily are intended for counterparties who transact swaps regularly, and therefore they are used mainly for interbank swaps.

Standardization provides several important benefits, including lower legal costs for preparing and agreeing swap transactions, simpler administration, and improved market liquidity. This is because standardization makes it easier to assign swaps to other counterparties.

BBAIRS Terms

The British Bankers Association issued its *Recommended Terms and Conditions for London Interbank Interest Rate Swaps* or BBAIRS terms in 1985. These were intended to apply to interbank swaps of less than two years' maturity (traded in London), including currency swaps. BBAIRS terms provide definitions of financial terms and conditions, and sample provisions setting out the rights of enforcement in an event of default by the other counterparty. Swaps can be negotiated and confirmed as being subject to BBAIRS terms, thereby speeding the negotiating, confirmation and documentation process significantly.

BBAIRS terms also define the LIBOR index for use in fixing the floating interest rate in a swap. BBAIRS Interest Rate Settlement Rates are published daily, for each monthly maturity between one and 12 months and for most major currencies.

Megacorp Bank
Flyover House
Northway
London EC3

To: Europa Bank
        London Branch   Date: 8 February 2000
        Fenchurch Street   Ref: ABC023
        London EC3

CONFIRMATION OF CROSS-CURRENCY INTEREST RATE SWAP AGREEMENT

We hereby confirm particulars in respect of the following Cross Currency Interest Rate Swap Agreement entered into between us subject to the British Bankers' Association's Recommended Terms and Conditions (BBAIRS terms) dated August 1985.

Contract Date:	8 February 2000
Currency A:	Dollars
Currency B:	Euros
Currency A Payer:	Megacorp Bank
Currency B Payer:	Europa Bank
Direct/Broker:	Broker
Commencement Date:	14 February 2000
Maturity Date:	14 February 2002
Currency A Amount:	$10,000,000
Currency B Amount:	€8,300,000

Foreign Exchange Rate Reference:	N/A
Initial Exchange:	No
Currency A Rate:	6 months BBAIRS Settlement Rate
Currency A Payment:	N/A
Currency A Payment Dates:	14/8/00 - 14/2/01 - 14/8/01 - 14/2/02
Currency B Rate:	N/A
Currency B Payment:	6 months BBAIRS Settlement Rate
Currency B Payment Dates:	14/2/01 - 14/2/02
Variation to BBAIRS Terms:	None
Currency A Payer's Account:	A/c 1236789 with Hessenbank, Frankfurt
Currency B Payer's Account:	A/c 1987234 with AmerBank, New York

PLEASE TELEPHONE OR CABLE US IMMEDIATELY IF THE PARTICULARS OF THIS CONFIRMATION ARE NOT IN ACCORDANCE WITH YOUR UNDERSTANDING.

For   Megacorp Bank

D Smith

Group Treasurer

Guidelines for Negotiating Terms

Dealing in the foreign exchange markets to buy or sell currency calls for quick decisions because exchange rates are held for only a short time and are continually fluctuating. In contrast, the arrangement of a swap transaction does not have the same time pressure. A large company wishing to arrange a swap will select a bank; the bank should be chosen for its expertise in swaps (and its credit strength). Major swaps banks include Citigroup, Deutsche Bank, Goldman Sachs and Morgan Stanley, and Barclays.

There are several steps for arranging a swap. First, the company should explain to the bank, preferably well in advance, what its requirements are and what swap structure is required. The bank will want to know

- the initial amount of principal to be supplied
- the exchange rate basis – spot, forward or some other defined rate
- the other currency involved
- the maturity of the swap
- the interest rate basis – fixed X into floating Y, fixed X into fixed Y or floating X into floating Y (where X is the initial currency and Y is the currency into which the initial currency is to be exchanged)
- the approximate timing of the swap transaction – whether same afternoon, next day or next week, etc.
- the quotation basis. The customer could ask for a quotation in cash amounts of interest rather than rates of interest payable and receivable, to avoid any misunderstanding about bond basis/moneymarket basis or six-monthly/annual rates.

Often it is worth going to competitive tender, and asking four or five swaps banks to quote prices immediately prior to transacting the swap. A company should stipulate to each of the swaps banks the exact exchange rate it requires for the exchange of principal. If the required basis is spot, the company should pick the spot rate at one point in time and quote it to all banks. Otherwise a fair price comparison is impossible.

Having asked one bank to quote at, for example, a dollar/yen spot rate of ¥120.00, the rate could have moved to ¥121.20 by the time the second bank was approached a minute later. This change would then affect the interest-rate exchange amounts.

When asking banks to quote, a company has a duty to respond as soon as possible. If it wants to try to improve on the pricing, it should either start the process again with fresh banks or approach one of the banks (with the best or second-best quote) and suggest it reprices at a stipulated level. Whether the bank's response is favorable or not, the company should immediately conclude or decline the transaction. It should not go through the entire list of banks again talking them down in price.

Having agreed to a transaction, the swaps bank will send confirmation to the company that should check the details carefully and query any apparent error. An example of confirmation is shown on page 109.

Costs of Arranging a Swap
No arrangement fee is charged for a swap because banks will earn their income from the interest rate differentials in the fixed rate quoted to counterparties.

Consequences of Default

For each party to a swap, there is some credit exposure to the counterparty. The credit risk is that the counterparty will fail to make an interest payment or will fail to re-exchange principal at the end of the swap's term. The consequence of such a failure would require replacing the missing cash flows at market prices. For example, if a company is receiving fixed sterling at 8% per annum against dollar LIBOR, and its swap bank fails to make an interest payment, the company would have to buy sterling with dollars to replace the missing cash flow, and would have to pay spot FX market rates to buy the sterling it requires.

The amount of a swap party's credit exposure to the counterparty in the swap includes the difference between

- cash inflows expected over the remaining term of the swap, and
- the cost of replacing these cash flows at current market rates, in the event of the counterparty defaulting on its payment obligations.

These cash flow differences over the remaining term of the swap can be valued at a present value amount by means of discounting. Depending on current market rates a credit risk could be negative because it would benefit one swap party if the counterparty were, for some reason, to default.

A second element in the credit exposure is the risk from the change in the exchange rate since the swap was transacted.

Example

Globe Bank makes a five-year swap transaction with a five-year bond issue. It issues $100 million in bonds and in the swap is a payer of fixed Swiss francs against dollar LIBOR. The exchange rate for the swap is SFr1.50 = $1. At the end of the three years the other counterparty defaults on the re-exchange of principal.

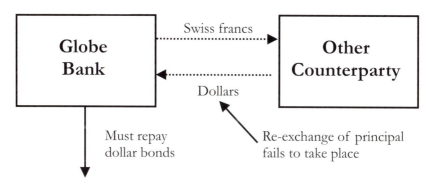

Analysis

Globe Bank must buy $100 million on the spot market to repay bondholders because of the swap counterparty's default. It had anticipated that the cost of obtaining the dollars would be SFr150 million in the re-exchange of principal under the swap agreement. If the spot market rate is now SFr1.40 = $1, the cost of buying the dollars would be SFr140 million, and Globe Bank would have a gain of SFr10 million, or $7.14 million from the counterparty's default. However, if the exchange is now SFr1.60 = $1, it would cost SFr160 million to buy the dollars and there would be a loss of SFr10 million, or $6.25 million.

Therefore the overall credit risk is the combination of an interest rate risk and a currency risk. A bank that transacts swaps with a customer is granting credit and the customer is using up some of its credit line with the bank. (Capital adequacy regulations for banks, under the Basle Agreement, specify the amount of capital a bank must allocate to credit exposures on its currency swaps.) Banks therefore will be reluctant to make a swap transaction with a counterparty that appears to be a credit risk, unless security or guarantees are given.

Conclusion

The swaps market received a stimulus in the 1980s from the continuing volatility of interest rates and exchange rates, combined with the development of international capital markets. Currency swaps help organizations to exploit opportunities in the markets to borrow more cheaply. They also can be used to hedge against long-term currency exposures.

It remains to be seen how far currency swaps will develop in the future. The main reasons for their use actually restrict their potential for development outside banks and large organizations.

- They can be used with bond issues to reduce the cost of borrowing, but this is appropriate only for companies large enough to contemplate a bond issue.
- They can be used to hedge long-term currency exposures, but only large companies and institutions are likely to have such identifiable exposures.

Glossary

Amortizing Swap

Currency swap in which the principal amount is gradually reduced over the life of the swap (with periodic exchanges of principal between the two counterparties).

Arbitrage

Dealing in two or more markets at the same time (or in similar products in the same market) to take advantage of temporary mispricing in order to make a profit.

Asset Swap

A swap in which two parties exchange a stream of cash flows from an asset (e.g. an investment) into a different stream. With currency swaps, an asset swap involves the exchange of a stream of income in one currency for a stream of income in a second currency, over a term (typically) of two to 10 years.

Assignment

The sale of a swap to a new counterparty, or buyout of a swap by a new counterparty.

BBAIRS Terms

British Bankers Association's Recommended Terms and Conditions for London Interbank Interest Rate Swaps.

Bond Basis

Swap rate based on a 360-day year and 30-day calendar month. Swaps arranged in association with a bond issue will have swap rates quoted on a bond basis.

Counterparty
The other party to a contract or deal.

Counterparty Risk
Risk that the other party to a contract will fail to fulfil his/her contract obligations. With currency swaps, counterparty risk includes the risk of failure to make a due payment of interest or principal (credit risk).

Credit Arbitrage
In the case of currency swaps, exploiting borrowing cost differences between two markets, to make a profit or gain. Credit arbitrage opportunities arise when two organizations each can borrow in two or more money/capital markets, but at interest rates that are comparatively better for one borrower in one market and for the other borrower in the other market.

Cross Currency Interest Rate Swap
A fixed rate against floating rate currency swap.

Currency Basis Swap
Swap involving the receipt (or payment) of a variable rate in one currency against payment (or receipt) of a variable rate in another, usually the dollar (e.g. floating sterling against dollar LIBOR).

Differential Swap
A type of currency basis swap where the notional principal amount is in just one currency, and interest payments are in one currency. However, interest payments are exchanged by reference to a floating rate index in one currency for one counterparty and to a floating rate index in a second currency for the other counterparty. One counterparty pays the other for the (floating rate) interest rate differential between the two currencies.

Eurobond

Marketable debt security issued outside the country in whose currency the debt is denominated.

Exposure

A term referring to the existence of a risk, e.g. currency exposure, credit exposure, interest rate exposure.

Fixed Rate

An interest rate that does not vary during the lifetime of a transaction (e.g. a loan or swap).

Floating Rate

An interest rate that is re-set at agreed intervals during the lifetime of a transaction (e.g. a loan or swap).

Forward Swap

Transaction in the FX markets involving the purchase (or sale) of a quantity of currency (spot) and the simultaneous forward sale of the same amount of currency.

Generic Swap

A swap with standard terms and no modifications.

Hedge

Action or instrument for reducing or eliminating risk.

ISDA

International Swaps and Derivatives Association that provides standardized documentation, conditions and procedures for swaps administration.

Liability Swap

A swap in which a counterparty exchanges a stream of cash outflows for a liability (e.g. a loan) into a different stream of outflows. With currency swaps, a liability swap involves the exchange of a stream of payments in one currency for a stream of payments in a second currency, over a term of (typically) two to 10 years.

Money Market Basis

Swap rate based on the actual number of days in a year (365 or 366). Swaps arranged with floating rate interest normally will have swap rates quoted on this basis.

Multi-Legged Swap

A number of swap agreements arranged by a bank, in which the requirements of other counterparties to the swaps can be matched, leaving the bank with little or no interest rate or currency exposures of its own.

Over-the-Counter Transaction

A transaction arranged by direct negotiation, usually by telephone, rather than through trading on an exchange.

Par Swap

A swap transacted with zero value (i.e. with no special risk features). A non-par swap has a value.

Plain Vanilla Swap

See Generic Swap.

Present Value

A valuation in today's money of a stream of future cash flows, after allowing for interest costs. Present value calculations are based on the premise that $1 in a future year is worth less than $1 now, because less than $1 needs to be invested now to yield $1 in a future year (the result of money's interest-earning capability over time). All cash flows in future years can be reduced to a present value equivalent, to assess investment yield potential or yield requirements.

Reversal

Eliminating the risk on an existing swap by transacting a second swap in the opposite direction.

Spread

The rate quoted on fixed rate payments or receipts can be either an absolute or a spread above the yield from an agreed fixed rate instrument, such as US Treasury bonds or UK gilts. The spread is the difference between the absolute price and the government bond yield.

Swap

An agreement between two parties to exchange a series of future payments. In a currency swap, the exchange of payments (cash flows) are in two currencies, one of which is often the dollar.

Swap Rate

The interest rate in a swap agreement, on which the regular exchange of cash flows during the term of the swap is based. Strictly speaking, a swap rate is not an interest rate because a swap involves the exchange of cash flows, not the exchange of loans or investments.

Zero Coupon Swap

Swap in which there are no exchanges of interest payments until maturity. (Interest is rolled up and becomes payable at maturity.)

Index

Notes

Notes